# THE NORMANS IN
# EUROPEAN HISTORY

# THE NORMANS IN
# EUROPEAN HISTORY

BY

CHARLES HOMER HASKINS

BARNES
&NOBLE
BOOKS
NEW YORK

TO MY WIFE

*Originally published in 1915.*

This edition published by Barnes & Noble, Inc.

1995 Barnes & Noble Books

ISBN 1-56619-783-X

Printed and bound in the United States of America

M 9 8 7 6 5 4 3 2 1

# PREFACE

THE eight lectures which are here published were delivered before the Lowell Institute in February, 1915, and at the University of California the following July, and it has seemed best to print them in the form in which they were prepared for a general audience. Their purpose is not so much to furnish an outline of the annals of Norman history as to place the Normans in relation to their time and to indicate the larger features of their work as founders and organizers of states and contributors to European culture. Biographical and narrative detail has accordingly been subordinated in the effort to give a general view of Norman achievement in France, in England, and in Italy. Various aspects of Norman history have been treated with considerable fullness by historians, but, so far as I am aware, no connected account of the whole subject has yet been attempted from this point of view. This fact, it is hoped, may justify the publication of these lectures, as well as explain the omission of many topics which would naturally be treated in an extended narrative.

This book rests partly upon the writings of the various scholars enumerated in the bibliographical note at the end of each chapter, partly upon prolonged personal investigations, the results of which have appeared in various special periodicals and will, in part, soon be collected into a volume of *Studies in Norman Institutions*. When it seemed appropriate in the text, I have felt at liberty to draw freely upon the more general portions of these articles, leaving more special and critical problems for discussion elsewhere.

I wish to thank the authorities of the Lowell Institute and the University of California, and to acknowledge helpful criticism from my colleague Professor William S. Ferguson and from Mr. George W. Robinson, Secretary of the Graduate School of Arts and Sciences of Harvard University. My indebtedness to Norman scholars and Norman scholarship is deeper and more personal than any list of their names and writings can indicate.

CHARLES H. HASKINS.

CAMBRIDGE, MASS.
*August*, 1915.

# CONTENTS

# THE NORMANS IN
# EUROPEAN HISTORY

## I

### NORMANDY AND ITS PLACE IN HISTORY

IN June, 1911, at Rouen, Normandy celebrated the one-thousandth anniversary of its existence. Decorated with the grace and simplicity of which only a French city is capable, the Norman capital received with equal cordiality the descendants of the conquerors and the conquered — Norwegians and Swedes, Danes of Denmark and Danes of Iceland, Normans of Normandy and of England, of Sicily and of Canada. Four Norwegian students accomplished the journey from their native fjords in an open Viking boat, having set ashore early in the voyage a comrade who had so far fallen away from the customs of his ancestors as to sleep under a blanket. From the United States bold Scandinavians, aided by the American Express Company, brought from Minnesota the Kensington rune stone, which purports to prove the presence of Norse explorers in the northwest one hundred and thirty years before the landfall of Columbus. A congress of Norman history listened for nearly a week in five simultaneous sections to communications on every phase of the Norman past. There was Norman music in the streets, there were Norman plays at the theatres, Norman mysteries in the cathedral close. Banquet followed banquet and toast followed toast, till the cider of Normandy paled before the champagne of France. Finally a great pageant, starting, like the city, from the river-bank, unrolled the vast panorama of Norman history through streets whose very names reëcho its great figures— Rollo and his Norse companions arriving in their Viking ships, the dukes his successors, William Longsword, Richard the Fearless, Robert the Magnificent, William the Conqueror, the sons of Tancred of Hauteville who drove the paynim from Sicily, and that other Tancred who planted the banner of the cross on the walls of Jerusalem, all with their knights and heralds and men at arms, followed by another pageant of the achievements of Normandy in the arts of peace. And on the last evening the great abbey-church of Saint-Ouen burnt red fire for the first time in its history till the whole mass glowed and every statue and storied niche stood out with some clear, sharp bit of the Norman past, while its lantern-tower, "the crown of Normandy," shone out over the city and the river which are the centre of Norman history and where this day the dukes wore again their crown.

In this transitory world the thousandth anniversary of anything is sufficiently rare to challenge attention, even in an age which is rapidly becoming hardened to.

celebrations. Of the events commemorated in 1915 the discovery of the Pacific is only four hundred years old, the signing of the Great Charter but seven hundred. The oldest American university has celebrated only its two hundred and fiftieth anniversary, the oldest European only its eight-hundredth. Even those infrequent commemorations which carry us back a thousand years or more, like the millenary of King Alfred or the sixteen-hundredth Constantinian jubilee of 1913, are usually reminders of great men or great events rather than, as in the case of Normandy, the completion of a millennium of continuous historical development. So far as I can now recollect, the only parallel is that of Iceland, which rounded out its thousand years with the dignity of a new constitution in 1874. Of about the same age, Iceland also resembles Normandy in being the creation of the Norse sea-rovers, an outpost of the Vikings in the west, as Normandy was an outpost in the south. Of the two, Iceland is perhaps the more individual, as it certainly has been the more faithful to its Scandinavian traditions, but the conditions which have enabled it to retain its early characteristics have also isolated it from the broader currents of the world's history. Normandy, on the other hand, was drawn at once into the full tide of European politics and became itself a founder of new states, an imperial power, a colonizer of lands beyond the seas, the mother of a greater Normandy in England, in Sicily, and in America.

At home and abroad the history of Normandy is a record of rich and varied achievement — of war and conquest and feats of arms, but also of law and government and religion, of agriculture, industry, trade, and exploration, of literature and science and art. It takes us back to Rollo and William of the Long Sword, to the Vikings and the Crusaders, to the conquerors of England and Sicily, to masterful prelates of the feudal age like Odo of Bayeux and Thomas Becket; it brings us down to the admirals and men of art and letters of the *Grand Siècle*, — Tourville and DuQuesne, Poussin, Malherbe, and the great Corneille, — to Charlotte Corday and the days of the Terror, and to the painters and scholars and men of letters of the nineteenth century, — Géricault and Millet, Laplace and Léopold Delisle, Flaubert and Maupassant and Albert Sorel. It traces the laborious clearing of ancient forests, the rude processes of primitive agriculture, the making of Norman cider and the breeding of the Norman horse, the vicissitudes of trade in fish and marten-skins, in pottery, cheap cottons, and strong waters, the development of a centre of fashion like Trouville or centres of war and commerce like Cherbourg and Havre. It describes the slow building of monasteries and cathedrals and the patient labors of priests and monks, as well as the conquest of the Canaries, the colonization of Canada, and the exploration of the Great West. A thousand years of such history are well worth a week of commemoration and retrospect.

To the American traveller who wends his way toward
Paris from Cherbourg, Havre, or Dieppe, the first impression of Normandy is that of a country strikingly
like England. There are the same high chalk cliffs, the
same "little grey church on the windy shore," often the
same orchards and hedges, poppies and roses. There are
trees and wide stretches of forest as in few other parts of
France, placid, full-brimmed rivers and quiet country-
sides, and everywhere the rich green of meadow and
park and pasture, that vivid green of the north which
made Alphonse Daudet at Oxford shudder, "Green
rheumatism," as he thought of the sun-browned plains
and sharp, bare hills of his own Provence. Normandy
is brighter than England, with a dash more of color in
the landscape, but its skies are not sunny and its air
breathes the mists of the sea and the chill of the north.
There is a grey tone also, of grey towns and grey sea,
matched by an austere and sombre element in the Norman character, which, if it does not take its pleasures
sadly after the manner of Taine's Englishmen, is prone
to take them soberly, and by an element of melancholy,
a sense of *le glas des choses mortes*, which Flaubert called
the melancholy of the northern barbarians. The Norman landscape also gives us the feeling of finish and re-
pose and the sentiment of a rich past, not merely in the
obvious externals of crumbling wall and ivied tower,
but in that deeper sense of a people bound from im-
memorial antiquity to the soil, adapted to every local

difference through long generations of use and wont, in
an intimate union of man and nature which makes the
Norman inseparable from his land. All this, too, is
English, but English with a difference. Just as, in
Henry James's phrase, the English landscape is a
landlord's landscape, and the French a peasant's, so
the *mairie* and the *préfecture*, the public garden and
the public band, the café and the ever-open church, the
workman's *blouse* and the grandam's *bonnet*, remind us
continually that we are in a Latin country and on our
way to Paris.

Now the history of Normandy reflects this twofold
impression of the traveller: it faces toward England and
the sea, but it belongs to France and the land. Open to
the outer world by the great valley of the Seine and the
bays and inlets of its long coast-line, Normandy was
never drawn to the sea in the same degree as its neighbor Brittany, nor isolated in any such measure from the
life of the Continent. Where the shore is low, meadow
and field run to the water's edge; where it is high, its
line is relatively little broken, so that the streams generally rush to the sea down short, steep valleys, up which
wheeze the trains which connect the little seaside ports
and watering-places with the modern world within. In
spite of the trade of its rivers and its ports, in spite of
the growth of industry along its streams, Normandy is
still primarily an agricultural country, rooted deep in
the rich soil of an ancient past, a country of horses and

cattle, of butter and cheese and cider and the kindly fruits of the earth; and the continuity of its history rests upon the land itself. "Behind the shore and even upon it," says Vidal de la Blache, "the ancient cumulative force of the interior has reacted against the sea. There an old and rich civilization has subsisted in its entirety, founded on the soil, through whose power have resisted and endured the speech, the traditions, and the peoples of ancient times."[1] Conquered and colonized by the sea-rovers of the north, the land of Normandy was able to absorb its conquerors into the law, the language, the religion, and the culture of France, where, as Sorel says, their descendants now preserve "their attachment to their native soil, the love of their ancestors, the respect for the ruins of the past, and the indestructible veneration for its tombs."[2]

If the character of Normandy is thus in considerable measure determined by geography, its boundaries and even its internal unity are chiefly the result of history. For good and ill, Normandy has, on the land side, no natural frontiers. The hills of the west continue those of Brittany, the plains of the east merge in those of Picardy. The watershed of the south marks no clear-cut boundary from Maine and Perche; the valleys of the Seine and the Eure lead straight to the Ile-de-France, separated from Normandy only by those border fortresses of the Avre and the Vexin which are the perpetual

[1] *La France*, p. 161.      [2] *Pages normandes*, dedication.

battle-ground of Norman history — Normandy's Alsace-Lorraine! Within these limits lie two distinct physiographic areas, one the lower portion of the Paris basin, the other a western region which belongs with Brittany and the west of France. These districts are commonly distinguished as Upper and Lower Normandy, terms consecrated by long use and representing two contrasted regions and types, but there is no general agreement as to their exact limits or the limits of the region of Middle Normandy which some have placed between them. Even the attempt to define these areas in terms of cheese — as the land respectively of the creamy Neufchâtel, the resilient Pont-l'Évêque, and the flowing Camembert — is defective from the point of view of geographical accuracy!

The most distinctive parts of Upper Normandy are the valley of the Seine and the region to the north and east, the *pays de Caux*, fringed by the coast from Havre to the frontier of Picardy. Less monotonous than the bare plains farther east, the plateau of Caux is covered by a rich vegetation, broken by scattered farmsteads, where house and orchard and outbuildings are protected from the wind by those rectangular earthworks surmounted by trees which are the most characteristic feature of the region. It is the country of *Madame Bovary* and of Maupassant's peasants. Equally typical is the valley of the Seine, ample, majestic, slow, cutting its sinuous way through high banks which grow higher

as we approach the sea, winding around ancient strongholds like Château Gaillard and Tancarville or ruined
abbeys like Jumièges and Saint-Wandrille, — where
Maeterlinck's bees still hum in the garden, — catching
the tide soon after it enters Normandy, reaching deep
water at Rouen, and meeting the "longed-for dash of
waves" in the great estuary at its mouth. Halfway from
the Norman frontier to the river's end stands Rouen,
mistress of the Seine and capital, not only of Upper Normandy, but of the whole Norman land. Celtic in name
and origin, like most French cities, chief town of the
Roman province of *Lugdunensis Secunda* and of the
ecclesiastical province to which this gave rise, the political and commercial importance of Rouen have made it
also the principal city of mediæval and modern Normandy and the seat of the changing political authority
to which the land has bowed. As early as the twelfth
century it is one of the famous cities of Europe, likened
to Rome by local poets and celebrated even by sober
historians for its murmuring streams and pleasant
meadows, its hill-girt site and strong defences, its beautiful churches and private dwellings, its well-stocked
markets, and its extensive foreign trade. In spite of all
modern changes, Rouen is still a city full of history, in
the parchments of its archives and the stones of its walls,
in its stately cathedral with the ancient tombs of the
Norman dukes, in the glorious nave of its great abbey-
church, the florid Gothic of Saint-Maclou, the richly

carved perpendicular of its Palace of Justice, and its splendid façades of the French Renaissance; historic also in those unbuilt spots which mark the landing of the Northmen and the burning of Joan of Arc.

Lower Normandy shows greater variety, comprising the hilly country of the Bocage, — the so-called Norman Switzerland, — the plain of Caen and the pasture-lands of the Bessin, and the wide sweep of the Atlantic coast-line, from the promontory of La Hague to the shifting sands of the bay of Mont-Saint-Michel. It is a country of green fields and orchards and sunken lanes, of dank parks and mouldering châteaux, of deserted mills and ancient parish churches, of quaint timbered houses and long village streets, of silent streams, small ports, and pebbly beaches, the whole merging ultimately in the neighboring lands of Brittany and Maine. Its typical places are Falaise, Vire, and Argentan, with their ancient castles of the Norman dukes; Bayeux and Coutances, the foundations of whose soaring cathedrals carry us back to the princely prelates of the Conquest; provincial capitals of the Old Régime, like Valognes, or the new, like Saint-Lô; and best of all, the crowning glories of the marvel of Mont-Saint-Michel. Its chief town is Caen, stern and grey, the heart of Normandy as Rouen is its head, an old poet tells us; no ancient Roman capital, but the creation of the mediæval dukes, who reared its great abbey-churches to commemorate the marriage and the piety of William the Conqueror

and Matilda, and who established their exchequer in
its castle; an intellectual centre also, the seat of the only
Norman university, of an academy, and of a society of
antiquaries which has recovered for us great portions
of the Norman past.

Fashioned and enriched by the hand of man, the land
of Normandy has in turn profoundly influenced the
character of its inhabitants. First and foremost, the
Norman is a peasant, industrious, tenacious, cautious,
secretive, distrustful of strangers, close-fisted, shrewd,
even to the point of cunning, a hard man at a bargain,
eager for gain, but with the genius for small affairs
rather than for great, for labor and economy rather
than enterprise and daring. Suspicious of novelty, he is
a conservative in politics with a high regard for vested
interests. The possession of property, especially landed
property, is his great ambition; and since, as St. Francis
long ago reminded us, property is the sower of strife and
suits at law, he is by nature litigious and lawyerly. There
is a well-known passage of Michelet which describes the
Norman peasant on his return from the fields explaining the Civil Code to his attentive children; Racine, who
immortalized Chicaneau in his *Plaideurs*, laid the scene
in a town of Lower Normandy. Even in his time this
was no new trait, for the fondness for legal form and
chicane can be traced in the early days of the *Coutume
de Normandie*, while the *Burnt Njal Saga* shows us the
love of lawsuits and fine points of procedure full-blown

among the Northmen of primitive Iceland. If Normandy is the *pays de gain*, it is also the *pays de sapience*. Hard-headed and practical, the Norman is not an idealist or a mystic; even his religion has a practical flavor, and the Bretons are wont to assert that there has never been a Norman saint. With the verse of Corneille and the splendid monuments of Romanesque and Gothic architecture before us, no one can accuse the Normans of lack of artistic sense, yet here, too, the Norman imagination is inclined to be restrained and severe, realistic rather than romantic. Its typical modern writers are Flaubert and Maupassant; its typical painter is Millet, choosing his scenes from Barbizon, but loyal to the peasant types of his native Normandy. Indeed Henry Adams insists that Flaubert's style, exact, impersonal, austere, is singularly like that of those great works of Norman Romanesque, the old tower of Rouen cathedral and St. Stephen's abbey at Caen, and shows us "how an old art transmutes itself into a new one, without changing its methods." [1] In history, a field in which the Norman attachment to the past has produced notable results, the distinguishing qualities of Norman work have been acute criticism and great erudition rather than brilliant imagination. In science, when a great Norman like Laplace discovered the nebular hypothesis, he relegated it to a note in the appendix to his ordered and systematic treatise on the

[1] *Mont-Saint-Michel and Chartres*, p. 55.

motions of the heavenly bodies. The Norman mind is neither nebular nor hypothetical!

The land is not the whole of nature's gift to Normandy; we must also take account of the sea, of those who came by sea and those who went down to the sea in ships; and history tells us of another type of Norman, those giants of an elder day who, as one of their descendants has said, "found the seas too narrow and the land too tame." The men who subdued England and Sicily, who discovered the Canaries and penetrated to the Mississippi, who colonized Quebec and ruled the Isle of France, were no stay-at-homes, no cautious landsmen interested in boundaries and inheritances and vain strivings about the law. Warriors and adventurers in untamed lands and upon uncharted seas, they were organizers of states and rulers of peoples, and it is their work which gives Normandy its chief claim upon the attention of the student of general history. These are the Normans of history and the Normans of romance. Listen to the earliest characterizations of them which have reached us from the south, as a monk of the eleventh century, Aimé of Monte Cassino, sets out to recount the deeds of the southern Normans, *fortissime gent* who have spread themselves over the earth, ever leaving small things to acquire greater, unwilling to serve, but seeking to have every one in subjection;[1] or as his contemporary, Geoffrey Malaterra,

---

[1] *Ystoire de li Normant* (ed. Delarc), p. 10.

himself very likely of Norman origin, describes this cunning and revengeful race, despising their own inheritance in the hope of winning a greater elsewhere, eager for gain and eager for power, quick to imitate whatever they see, at once lavish and greedy; given to hunting and hawking and delighting in horses and accoutrements and fine clothing, yet ready when occasion demands to bear labor and hunger and cold; skilful in flattery and the use of fine words, but unbridled unless held down firmly by the yoke of justice.[1] Turn then to the northern writers of the following century: William of Malmesbury, who describes the fierce onslaughts of the Normans, inured to war and scarcely able to live without it, their stratagems and breaches of faith and their envy of both equals and superiors;[2] or the English monk Ordericus, who spent his life among them in Normandy and who says: —

The race of the Normans is unconquered and ready for any wild deed unless restrained by a strong ruler. In whatever gathering they find themselves they always seek to dominate, and in the heat of their ambition they are often led to violate their obligations. All this the French and Bretons and Flemings and other neighbors have frequently felt; this the Italians and the Lombards, the Angles and Saxons, have also learned to their undoing.[3]

A little later it is the Norman poet Wace who tells, through the mouth of the dying William the Con-

---

[1] *Historia Sicula*, I, 3.  [2] *Gesta Regum* (Rolls Series), p. 306.
[3] Ed. LePrévost, III, p. 474; cf. p. 230.

queror, of these same Normans — brave and valiant
and conquering, proud and boastful and fond of good
cheer, hard to control and needing to be kept under
foot by their rulers.[1] Through all these accounts runs
the same story of a high-spirited, masterful, unscrupulous race, eager for danger and ready for every adventure, and needing always the bit and bridle rather than
the spur.

The contrast is not merely between the eleventh century and the twentieth, between a lawless race of pioneers and a race subdued and softened by generations of
order and peace; the two types are present in the early
days of Norman history. Among the conquerors of
England a recent historian distinguishes "the great
soldiers of the invading host . . . equally remarkable
for foresight in council and for headlong courage in the
hour of action, whose wits are sharpened by danger and
whose resolution is only stimulated by obstacles; incapable of peaceful industry but willing to prepare
themselves for war and rapine by the most laborious
apprenticeship"; and over against them "the politi-
cians . . . cautious, plausible, deliberate, with an im-
mense capacity for detail, and an innate liking for routine; conscious in a manner of their moral obligations,
but mainly concerned with small economies and gains;
limited in their horizon, but quick to recognise superior
powers and to use them for their own objects; indifferent

[1] *Roman de Rou* (ed. Andresen), II, lines 9139–56.

for their own part to high ideals, and yet respectful to idealists; altogether a hard-headed, heavy-handed, laborious and tenacious type of men." [1]

These contrasting types of life and character it is tempting to refer to the respective influences of land and water, to the differences between the peasant and the rider to the sea. One might even attempt a philosophy of Norman history somewhat on this wise. In its normal and undisturbed state Normandy is a part of France, in its life as in its geography, and as such it shows only the ordinary local differences from the rest of the French lands. So it was under the Romans, so under the Franks. At the beginning of the tenth century the coming of the Northmen introduces a new element which develops relations with the sea and the countries beyond the sea, with Scandinavia and later with the British Isles. Normandy ceases to be provincial, it almost ceases to be French; it even becomes the centre of an Atlantic empire which stretches from Scotland to the Pyrenees. It sends its pilgrims to Compostela, its chivalry to Jerusalem, its younger sons to Sicily and southern Italy. Its relations with the sea do not cease with its political separation from the lands across the Channel in 1204. The English come back for a time in the fifteenth century; the Normans cross the Atlantic in the sixteenth and settle Canada in the seventeenth. But the overmastering influence of the soil

[1] H. W. C. Davis, *England under the Normans and Angevins*, p. 3.

prevails and draws its children back to itself. The sea-faring impulse declines; activity turns inward; the province is finally absorbed in the nation; Normandy is again a part of France, and the originality and distinctness of its history fade away in the life of the whole.

Philosophy or no philosophy, the history of Normandy falls for our purposes into three convenient periods. The first of these extends from the earliest times to the coming of the Northmen in 911, the event which created Normandy as a distinct entity. The second is the history of the independent Norman duchy from 911 to the French conquest in 1204, the three splendid centuries of Norman independence and Norman greatness. The third period of seven hundred years deals with Normandy as a part of France.

The interest and importance of these several periods vary with the point of view. Many people are of the opinion that the only history which matters is modern history, and the more modern the better because the nearer to ourselves and our time. To such everything is meaningless before the French Revolution or the Franco-Prussian War— or perhaps the War of 1914. To those who care only for their own time the past has no perspective; as a distinguished maker and writer of history has said, James Buchanan and Tiglath-Pileser become contemporaries. This foreshortened interest in the immediate past starts from a sound principle, namely, that it is an important function of history to explain the present in the light of the past from which it has come. By a natural reaction from the study which stopped with Marcus Aurelius or the American colonies or the Congress of Vienna, the demand naturally arose for the history of the day before yesterday, which was once declared to be the least known period in human annals. This is quite legitimate if it does not stop here and does not accept the easy assumption that what is nearest us is necessarily most important, even to ourselves. Modern Germany owes more to Martin Luther than to Nietzsche, more to Charles the Great, who eleven hundred years ago conquered and civilized the Saxons and began the subjugation of the Slavs, than to many a more modern figure in the Sieges-allee at Berlin. Our method of reckoning time and latitude by sixtieths owes less to the contemporaries of James Buchanan than to those of Tiglath-Pileser. If we must apply material standards to history, we must consider the mass as well as the square of the distance.

Obviously, too, we must consider distance in space as well as in time. The Boston fire of 1872 did not rouse Paris, and our hearts do not thrill at the mention of the Socialist mayors and Conservative deputies whose names become household words when the streets of French towns are rechristened in their memory. The perspective of Norman history is different for a Norman

than for other Frenchmen, different for a Frenchman
than for an American.

Now there can be no question that for the average
Norman the recent period bulks larger than the earlier.
His life is directly and constantly affected by the bureaucratic traditions of the Old Régime, by the new
freedom and the land-distribution of the Revolution,
by the coming of the railroad, the steamship, and the
primary school. William the Conqueror, Philip Augustus, Joan of Arc, their deeds and their times, have become mere traditions to him, if indeed they are that.
In all these changes, however, there is nothing distinctive, nothing peculiar, nothing that cannot be studied
just as well in some other part of France. Their local
and specifically Norman aspects are of absorbing interest to Normandy, but they are meaningless to the
world at large. With the union with France in 1204
Norman history becomes local history, and whatever
possesses more than local interest it shares with the
rest of France. From the point of view of the world
at large, the history of Normandy runs parallel with
that of the other regions of France. Normandy will
contribute its quota of great names to the world, in
art and music and literature, in learning and industry and politics; it will take its part in the great
movements of French history, the Reformation, the
Revolution, the new republic; but it will be only a
part of a larger whole and derive its interest for the

general student from its membership in the body of France.

Much the same is true of the period before the coming of the Northmen. Under the Celts, the Romans, and the Franks, the region which was to become Normandy is not distinguished in any notable way from the rest of Gaul, and it has the further disadvantage of being one of the regions concerning which our knowledge is particularly scanty. A few names of tribes in Cæsar's *Gallic War* and in the Roman geographers, a few scattered inscriptions from the days of the empire, a few lives of saints and now and then a rare document of Frankish times, this with the results of archæological research constitutes the basis of early Norman history. After all, Normandy was remote from Rome and lay apart also from the main currents of Frankish life and politics, so that we should not look here for much light on general conditions. Nevertheless it is in this obscure age that the foundations of Normandy were laid. First of all, the population, Gallo-Roman at bottom, receiving a Germanic admixture of Saxons and Franks long before the coming of the Northmen, but still preponderantly non-Germanic in its racial type. Next, language, determined by the process of Romanization and persisting as a Romance speech in spite of Saxon and Frank and Northman, until in the earliest monuments of the eleventh century we can recognize the beginnings of modern French. Then law, the Frankish law which the Northmen were to absorb, perpetuate, and carry to England. Fourth, religion, the Christian faith, triumphing only with difficulty in a land largely rural and open to barbarian invasion, but established firmly by the sixth century and already reënforced by monastic foundations which were to be the centres of faith and culture to a later age. Finally, the framework of political geography, resting on the Roman cities which with some modifications were perpetuated as the dioceses of the mediæval church, and connected by Roman roads which remained until modern times the great highways of local communication. A beginning was also made in the direction of separate organization when, toward the close of the fourth century, these districts of the northwest are for the first time set off by themselves as an administrative area, the province of *Lugdunensis Secunda*, which coincides with later Normandy. Then, as regularly throughout Gaul, the civil province becomes the ecclesiastical province, centring about its oldest church, Rouen, and the province of the archbishop of Rouen perpetuates the boundaries of the political area after the political authority passed away, and carries over to the Middle Ages the outline of the Roman organization. In all this process there is nothing particularly different from what took place throughout the greater part of northern Gaul, but the results were fundamental for Normandy and for the whole of Norman history.

A new epoch begins with the coming of the Northmen
in the early tenth century, as a result of which Normandy was differentiated from the rest of France and
carried into the broader currents of European history.
At first an outpost of the Scandinavian north, its relations soon shifted as it bred the conquerors of England and Sicily.  The Normans of the eleventh century,
Henry Adams maintains, stood more fully in the centre
of the world's history than their English descendants
ever did.  They "were a part, and a great part, of the
Church, of France, and of Europe."  The Popes leaned
on them, at times heavily.  By the conquest of England
the "Norman dukes cast the kings of France into the
shade. . . . Normans were everywhere in 1066, and
everywhere in the lead of their age."[1]  A century later
Normans ruled half of Italy, two thirds of France, and
the whole of England; and they had made a beginning
on Ireland and Scotland.  No one can write of European affairs throughout this whole period without
giving a large place to the Normans and their doings;
while events like the conquests of England and Ireland changed the course of history.

Normandy has also its place in the history of European institutions, for the Normans were organizers as
well as conquerors, and their political creations were
the most efficient states of their time.  Masterful, yet
legally minded and businesslike, with a sense for detail

[1] *Mont-Saint-Michel and Chartres*, p. 4.

and routine, the Norman princes had a sure instinct for state-building, at home and abroad. The Norman duchy was a compact and powerful state before its duke crossed the Channel, and the central government which the Normans created in England showed the same characteristics on a larger scale. The Anglo-Norman empire of the twelfth century was the marvel of its day, while the history of the Norman kingdom of Sicily showed that the Norman genius for assimilation and political organization was not confined to the dukes of Rouen. Highly significant during the eleventh and twelfth centuries, Norman institutions remained of permanent importance, affecting the central administration of France in ways which are still obscure, and exerting a decisive influence upon the law and government of England. Normandy was the connecting link between the Frankish law of the Continent and the English common law, and thus claims a share in the jurisprudence of the wide-flung lands to which the common law has spread. The institution of trial by jury, for example, is of Norman origin, or rather of Frankish origin and Norman development.

By virtue, then, of its large part in the events of its time, by virtue of the decisive character of the events in which the Normans took part, and by virtue of the permanent influence of its institutions, the Normandy of the dukes can claim an important position in the general history of the world. In seeking to describe the

place of the Normans in European history we shall accordingly pass over those periods, the earlier and the
later, which are primarily of local interest, and concentrate ourselves upon the heroic age of the tenth, eleventh, and twelfth centuries. We shall begin with the
coming of the Northmen and the creation of the Norman state. The third lecture will consider the Norman
conquest of England; the fourth, the Norman empire to
which this gave rise. We shall then trace the events
which led to the separation of Normandy from England
and its ultimate union in 1204 with the French monarchy under Philip Augustus, concluding our survey of
the Normans of the north by a sketch of Norman life
and culture in this period. The two concluding lectures
will trace the establishment of the Norman kingdom
of southern Italy and Sicily, and examine the brilliant
composite civilization of the southern Normans from the
reign of the great King Roger to the accession of his
still more famous grandson, the Emperor Frederick II.

## BIBLIOGRAPHICAL NOTE

There is no substantial general history of Normandy. For a review
of the materials, the literature, and the problems, see the excellent
résumé of H. Prentout, *La Normandie* (Paris, 1910, reprinted from
the *Revue de synthèse historique*). For bibliographical purposes this
should be supplemented by the *Catalogue des ouvrages normands de
la Bibliothèque municipale de Caen* (Caen, 1910-12). For the general
features of Norman geography, see the brief account by Vidal de la
Blache, in the *Histoire de France* of Lavisse, republished with illustrations under the title of *La France* (Paris, 1908). The subject can best

be followed out in J. Sion, *Les paysans de la Normandie orientale* (Paris, 1908), and R. de Félice, *La Basse-Normandie* (Paris, 1907). Various aspects of Norman genius and character are delightfully treated by Albert Sorel, *Pages normandes* (Paris, 1907). The proceedings of the historical congress held in conjunction with the millénaire of 1911 were to have been printed in full, but so far only various reprints of individual communications have appeared. J. Touflet, *Le millénaire de Normandie* (Rouen, 1913), is not an account of the commemoration, but an illustrated collection of popular papers. One of the more notable pamphlets published on this occasion is that of Gabriel Monod, *Le rôle de la Normandie dans l'histoire de France* (Paris, 1911).

## II

### THE COMING OF THE NORTHMEN

THE central fact of Norman history and the starting-point for its study is the event so brilliantly commemorated by the millenary of 1911, the grant of Normandy to Rollo and his northern followers in the year 911. The history of Normandy, of course, began long before that year. The land was there, and likewise in large measure the people, that is to say, probably the greater part of the elements which went to make the population of the country at a later day; and the history of the region can be traced back several centuries. But after all, neither the Celtic *civitates* nor the Roman province of *Lugdunensis Secunda* nor the ecclesiastical province of Rouen which took its place nor the northwestern *pagi* of the Frankish empire were Normandy. They lacked the name — that is obvious; they lacked also individuality of character, which is more. They were a part, and not a distinctive part, of something else, whereas later Normandy was a separate entity with a life and a history of its own. And the dividing line must be drawn when the Northmen first established themselves permanently in the land and gave it a new name and a new history.

It must be said that the date 911, like most exact

dates in history, is somewhat arbitrary. The Northmen first invaded Normandy in 841, and their inroads did not cease until about 966, so that the year 911 falls near the middle of a century and a quarter of invasion and settlement, and marks neither the beginning nor the end of an epoch. It is also true that this date, like many another which appears in heavy-faced type in our histories, is not known with entire certainty, for some historians have placed in 912 or even later the events commonly assigned to that year. On the whole, however, there is good reason for maintaining 911 — and a thousandth anniversary must have some definite date to commemorate!

For the actual occurrences of that year, we have only the account of a romancing historian of a hundred years later, reënforced here and there by the exceedingly scanty records of the time. The main fact is clear, namely that the Frankish king, Charles the Simple, granted Rollo as a fief a considerable part, the eastern part, of later Normandy. Apparently Rollo did homage for his fief in feudal fashion by placing his hands between the hands of the king, something, we are told, which "neither his father, nor his grandfather, nor his great-grandfather before him had ever done for any man." Legend goes on to relate, however, that Rollo refused to kneel and kiss the king's foot, crying out in his own speech, "No, by God!" and that the companion to whom he delegated the unwelcome obligation performed it so clumsily that he overturned the king, to the great merriment of the assembled Northmen. Rollo did not receive the whole of the later duchy, but only the region on either side of the Seine which came to be known as Upper Normandy, and it was not till 924 that the Northmen acquired also middle Normandy, or the Bessin, while the west, the Cotentin and the Avranchin, fell to them only in 933.

As to Rollo's personality, we have only the evidence of later Norman historians of doubtful authority and the Norse saga of Harold Fairhair. If, as seems likely, their accounts relate to the same person, he was known in the north as Hrolf the Ganger, because he was so huge that no horse could carry him and he must needs gang afoot. A pirate at home, he was driven into exile by the anger of King Harold, whereupon he followed his trade in the Western Isles and in Gaul, and rose to be a great Jarl among his people. The saga makes him a Norwegian, but Danish scholars have sought to prove him a Dane, and more recently the cudgels have been taken up for his Swedish origin. To me the Norwegian theory seems on the whole the most probable, being based on a trustworthy saga and corroborated by other incidental evidence. Yet, however significant of Rollo's importance it may be that three great countries should each claim him as its own, like the seven cities that strove for the honor of Homer's birthplace, the question of his nationality is historically of subordinate interest, and at a time when national lines were not yet drawn, it is futile to fit the inadequate evidence into one or another theory. The important fact is that Norway, Denmark, and even more distant Sweden, all contributed to the colonists who settled in Normandy under Rollo and his successors, and the achievements of the Normans thus become the common heritage of the Scandinavian race.

The colonization of Normandy was, of course, only a small part of the work of this heroic age of Scandinavian expansion. The great emigration from the North in the ninth and tenth centuries has been explained in part by the growth of centralized government and the consequent departure of the independent, the turbulent, and the untamed for new fields of adventure; but its chief cause was doubtless that which lies back of colonizing movements in all ages, the growth of population and the need of more room. Five centuries earlier this land-hunger had pushed the Germanic tribes across the Rhine and Danube and produced the great wandering of the peoples which destroyed the Roman empire; and the Viking raids were simply a later aspect of this same *Völkerwanderung*, retarded by the outlying position of the Scandinavian lands and by the greater difficulty of migration by sea. For, unlike the Goths who swept across the map of Europe in vast curves of marching men, or the Franks who moved forward by slow stages of gradual settlement in their occupation of Roman Gaul, the Scandinavian invaders were men of the sea and migrated in ships. The deep fjords of Norway and the indented coast of the North Sea and the Baltic made them perforce sailors and fishermen and taught them the mastery of the wider ocean. In their dragon ships — shallow, clinker-built, half-decked craft, pointed at either end, low in the middle, where the gunwale was protected by a row of shields — they could cross the sea, explore creeks and inlets, and follow the course of rivers far above their mouth. The greater ships might reach the length of seventy-five feet and carry as many as one hundred and twenty men, but these were the largest, and even these offered but a slow means of migration. We must think of the whole movement at first as one of small and scattered bands, terrible more for their fierce, sudden, and skilful methods of attack, than for force of superior numbers or organization. The truth is that sea-power, whose strategic significance in modern warfare Admiral Mahan did so much to make us appreciate, was in the ninth and tenth centuries, so far as western Europe was concerned, a Scandinavian monopoly. Masters of the seas, the Northmen harried the coasts and river-valleys as they would, and there was none to drive them back.

Outside of the Baltic, where the Danes ravaged the southern coast and the Swedes moved eastward to lay the foundations of the Russian state and to penetrate as far as Constantinople, two main routes lay open to the masters of the northern seas. One led west to the Orkneys, the Shetlands, and the coast of Scotland, and then either south to the shores of Ireland, or further west to Iceland, Greenland, and America. The other led through the North Sea to England, the Low Countries, and the coast of Gaul. Both were used, and used freely, by the Vikings, and in both directions they accomplished enduring results: — Iceland and the kingdoms of the isles in the north, the beginnings of town life and commerce in Ireland, the Danelaw in England, and the duchy of Normandy.

When the great northern invasions began at the close of the eighth century, Charles the Great ruled all the Christian lands of the western Continent. By fire and sword he converted the heathen Saxons of the north to Christianity and civilization and advanced his frontier to the Danish border, so that the pious monk of St. Gall laments that he did not conquer the Danes also — "be it that Divine Providence was not then on our side, or that our sins rose up against us." And this same gossiping chronicler — not the best of authorities it is true — has left us a striking picture of Charlemagne's first experience with the Scandinavian invaders: —

Once Charles arrived by chance at a certain maritime town of Gallia Narbonensis. While he was sitting at dinner, and had not been recognized by the townspeople, some northern pirates came to carry on their depredations in that very port. When the ships were perceived some thought they were Jewish merchants, some that they were Africans, some Bretons. But the wise king, knowing from the shape and swiftness of the vessels what sort of crews they carried, said to those about him, "These ships bear no merchandize, but cruel foes." At these words all the Franks rivalled each other in the speed with which they rushed to attack the boats. But it was useless. The Northmen hearing that there stood the man whom they were wont to call Charles the Hammer, were afraid lest all their fleet should be taken in the port, and should be broken in pieces; and their flight was so rapid, that they withdrew themselves not only from the swords, but even from the eyes of those who wished to catch them. The religious Charles, however, seized by a holy fear, rose from the table, and looked out of the window towards the East, remaining long in that position, his face bathed in tears. No one ventured to question him: but turning to his followers he said, "Know ye why I weep? Truly I fear not that these will injure *me*. But I am deeply grieved that in my lifetime they should have been so near landing on these shores, and I am overwhelmed with sorrow as I look forward and see what evils they will bring upon my offspring and their people." [1]

From the actuality of such an invasion the great Charles was spared, but in the British Isles it had already begun. In 787 the Anglo-Saxon *Chronicle* tells us there "first came three ships of Northmen out of Haeretha-land" [Denmark?], whereupon the reeve of the Dorset port "rode down to the place and would have driven them to the king's town, because he knew not who they were; and they there slew him. These were the first ships of Danishmen which sought the

---

[1] II, 14, as translated by Keary, *Vikings*, p. 136.

land of the English nation." Six years later they fell
upon the holy isle of Lindisfarne, pillaged the church
sacred with the memories of Northumbrian Christianity,
and slew the monks or drove them into the sea. In 807
they first landed in Ireland, and "after this there came
great sea-cast floods of foreigners into Erin, so that there
was not a point thereof without a fleet." Then came the
turn of the Continent, first along the coast of Frisia and
Flanders, and then in what is now France. In 841,
when the grandsons of Charlemagne were quarrelling
over the fragments of his empire at Fontenay, the first
fleet of Northmen entered the Seine; in 843 when they
were making their treaty of partition at Verdun, the
Vikings entered Nantes on St. John's Day and slew
the bishop before the high altar as he intoned the *Sur-
sum corda* of the mass. Within two years they sacked
Hamburg and Paris. Wherever possible they established
themselves at the mouths of the great rivers, often on
an island like Walcheren, Noirmoutier, or the Ile de
Rhé, whence the rivers opened the whole country to
them — Elbe and Weser, Rhine and Meuse, Scheldt,
Seine, Loire, and Garonne, even to the Guadalquivir, by
which the Arabic chronicler tells us the "dark red sea-
birds" penetrated to Seville. One band more venture-
some than the rest, entered the Mediterranean and
reached Marseilles, whence under their leader Hastings
they sacked the Italian town of Luna, apparently in the
belief that it was Rome.

About the middle of the ninth century the number of the Norse pirates greatly increased and their ravages became more regular and constant, leading in many cases to permanent settlements. In 855 the Old English *Chronicle* tells us "the heathen men, for the first time, remained over winter in Sheppey," at the mouth of the Thames, and thereafter, year by year, it recounts the deeds of the Viking band which wintered in England and is called simply *here*, the army. It is no longer a matter of summer raids but of unbroken occupation. In 878 during midwinter "the army stole away to Chippenham and overran the land of the West-Saxons and sat down there; and many of the people they drove beyond sea, and of the remainder the greater part they subdued and forced to obey them except King Alfred, and he, with a small band, with difficulty retreated to the woods and to the fastnesses of the moors." The following year a similar band, now swollen into "the great army" made its appearance on the Continent and for fourteen years ravaged the territory between the Rhine and the Loire. Year after year "the steel of the heathen glistened"; in 886 they laid siege to Paris, which was relieved not by the king's valor but by his offering them Burgundy to plunder instead. A century later the English began to buy them off with Danegeld. "All men," laments a chronicler, "give themselves to flight. No one cries out, Stand and fight for your country, your church, your countrymen. What they ought to defend with arms, they shamefully redeem by payments." There was nothing to do but add a new petition to the litany, "From the fury of the Northmen, good Lord, deliver us."

To the writers of the time, who could not see the permanent results of Viking settlement, the Northmen were barbarian pirates, without piety or pity, "who wept neither for their sins nor for their dead," and their expeditions were mere wanton pillage and destruction. Moreover, these writers were regularly monks or priests, and it was the church that suffered most severely. A walled town or castle might often successfully resist, but the monasteries, protected from Christian freebooters by their sacred character, were simply so many opportunities for plunder to the heathen of the north. Sometimes the monks perished with their monastery, often they escaped only with their lives and a few precious title-deeds, to find on their return merely a heap of blackened ruins and a desolate countryside. Many religious establishments utterly disappeared in the course of the invasions. In Normandy scarcely a church survives anterior to the tenth century. As the monasteries were at this time the chief centres of learning and culture throughout western Europe, their losses were the losses of civilization, and in this respect the verdict of the monastic chroniclers is justified. There is, however, another side to the story, which Scandinavian scholars have not been slow to emphasize. Heathen still and from one point of view barbarian, the Northmen had yet a culture of their own, well advanced on its material side, notable in its artistic skill, and rich in its treasures of poetry and story. Its material treasures have been in part recovered by the labors of northern archæologists, while its literary wealth is now in large measure accessible in English in the numerous translations of sagas and Eddic poems.

After all barbarism, like culture, is a relative thing, and judged by contemporary standards, the Vikings were not barbarians. They rather show a strange combination of the primitive and the civilized — elemental passions expressing themselves with a high degree of literary art, barbaric adornment wrought with skilled craftsmanship, Berserker rage supplemented by clever strategy, pitiless savagery combined with a strong sense of public order, constant feuds and murders coexistent with a most elaborate system of law and legal procedure. Young from our point of view, the civilization of the Vikings had behind it a history of perhaps fifteen centuries.

On its material side Viking civilization is characterized by a considerable degree of wealth and luxury. Much of this, naturally, was gained by pillage, but much also came by trade. The northern warriors do not seem to have had that contempt for traffic which has characterized many military societies, and they turned read-

ily enough from war to commerce. In a Viking tomb
recently discovered in the Hebrides there were found be-
side the sword and spear and battle-axe of all warriors,
a pair of scales, fit emblem of the double life the chief
had led on earth and may have hoped to continue hereafter! Of trade, and especially trade with the Orient,
there is abundant evidence in the great treasures of gold
and silver coin found in many regions of the north.
The finely wrought objects of gold and silver and en-
crusted metal, which were once supposed to have been
imported from the south and east, are now known
to have been in large part of native workmanship, influenced, of course, by the imitation of foreign models,
but also carrying out traditions of ornamentation, such
as the use of animal forms, which can be traced back
continuously to the earliest ages of Scandinavian history.
Shields and damascened swords, arm-rings and neck-
rings, pins and brooches — especially brooches, if you
find an unknown object, says Montelius, call it a brooch
and you will generally be right — all testify, both in
their abundance and their beauty of workmanship, to an
advanced stage of art and handicraft.

This love of the north for luxury of adornment is
amply seen in chronicle and saga. When the Irish drove
the Vikings out of Limerick in 968 they took from them
"their jewels and their best property, and their saddles
beautiful and foreign, their gold and their silver, their
beautifully woven cloth of all kinds and colors — satin

and silk, pleasing and variegated, both scarlet and green, and all sorts of cloth in like manner." "How," asks the Valkyrie in the *Lay of the Raven*, "does the generous Prince Harold deal with the men of feats of renown that guard his land?" The Raven answers: —

They are well cared for, the warriors that cast dice in Harold's court. They are endowed with wealth and with fair swords, with the ore of the Huns, and with maids from the East. They are glad when they have hopes of a battle, they will leap up in hot haste and ply the oars, snapping the oar-thongs and cracking the tholes. Fiercely, I ween, do they churn the water with their oars at the king's bidding.

*Quoth the Walkyrie:* I will ask thee, for thou knowest the truth of all these things, of the meed of the Poets, since thou must know clearly the state of the minstrels that live with Harold.

*Quoth the Raven:* It is easily seen by their cheer, and their gold rings, that they are among the friends of the king. They have red cloaks right fairly fringed, silver-mounted swords, and ring-woven sarks, gilt trappings, and graven helmets, wrist-fitting rings, the gifts of Harold.[1]

As regards social organization, Viking society shows the Germanic division into three classes, thrall, churl, and noble. Their respective characters and occupations are thus described in the *Rigsmal:* —

Thrall was of swarthy skin, his hands wrinkled, his knuckles bent, his fingers thick, his face ugly, his back broad, his heels long. He began to put forth his strength, binding bast, making loads, and bearing home faggots the weary long day. His children busied themselves with building

---

[1] *Corpus Poeticum Boreale,* I, p. 257.

fences, dunging plowland, tending swine, herding goats, and digging peat. Their names were Sooty and Cowherd, Clumsy and Lout and Laggard, etc. Carl, or churl, was red and ruddy, with rolling eyes, and took to breaking oxen, building plows, timbering houses, and making carts. Earl, the noble, had yellow hair, his cheeks were rosy, his eyes were keen as a young serpent's. His occupation was shaping the shield, bending the bow, hurling the javelin, shaking the lance, riding horses, throwing dice, fencing, and swimming. He began to waken war, to redden the field, and to fell the doomed.[1]

Both churl and earl were largely represented in those who went to sea, but the nobility naturally preponderated, and it is particularly their exploits which the sagas and poems celebrate. Viking warfare was no mere clash of swords; they conducted their military operations with skill and foresight, and showed great power of adapting themselves to new conditions, whether that meant the invasion of an open country or the siege of a fortified town. Much, however, must be credited to their *furor Teutonicus*, to that exuberance of military spirit which they had inherited from far-off ancestors. Not all were wolf-coated Bearsarks, but all seemed to have that delight in war and conflict for their own sakes which breathes through their poetry: —

The sword in the king's hand bit through the weeds of Woden [mail] as if it were whisked through water, the spearpoints clashed, the shields were shattered, the axes rattled on the heads of the warriors. Targets and skulls were trod-

[1] *Corpus Poeticum Boreale*, i, pp. 236–40.

den under the Northmen's shield-fires [weapons] and the hard heels of their hilts. There was a din in the island, the kings dyed the shining rows of shields in the blood of men. The wound-fires [blades] burnt in the bloody wounds, the halberds bowed down to take the life of men, the ocean of gore dashed upon the swords'-ness, the flood of the shafts fell upon the beach of Stord. Halos of war mixed under the vault of the bucklers; the battle-tempest blew underneath the clouds of the targets, the lees of the sword-edges [blood] pattered in the gale of Woden. Many a man fell into the stream of the brand.[1]

Again: —

Brands broke against the black targets, wounds waxed when the princes met. The blades hammered against the helm-crests, the wound-gravers, the sword's point, bit. I heard that there fell in the iron-play Woden's oak [heroes] before the swords [the sword-belt's ice].

*Second Burden:* There was a linking of points and a gnashing of edges: Eric got renown there.

*Second Stave:* The prince reddened the brand, there was a meal for the ravens; the javelin sought out the life of man, the gory spears flew, the destroyer of the Scots fed the steed of the witch [wolves], the sister of Nari [Hell] trampled on the supper of the eagles [corses]. The cranes of battle [shafts] flew against the walls of the sword [bucklers], the wound-mew's lips [the arrows' barbs] were not left thirsty for gore. The wolf tore the wounds, and the wave of the sword [blood] plashed against the beak of the raven.

*Third Burden:* The lees of the din of war [blood] fell upon Gialf's steed [ship]: Eric gave the wolves carrion by the sea.

*Third Stave:* The flying javelin bit, peace was belied there, the wolf was glad, and the bow was drawn, the bolts clattered, the spear-points bit, the flaxen-bowstring bore the

---

[1] *Corpus Poeticum Boreale*, I, p. 265 *f.*

arrows out of the bow. He brandished the buckler on his arm, the rouser of the play of blades — he is a mighty hero. The fray grew greater everywhere about the king. It was famed east over the sea, Eric's war-faring.[1]

Or listen to the weird sisters as they weave the web of Ireland's fate under Brian Boru: —

Wide-stretched is the warp presaging the slaughter, the hanging cloud of the beam; it is raining blood. The gray web of the hosts is raised up on the spears, the web which we the friends of Woden are filling with red weft.

This web is warped with the guts of men, and heavily weighted with human heads; blood-stained darts are the shafts, iron-bound are the stays; it is shuttled with arrows. Let us strike with our swords this web of victory!

War and Sword-clasher, Sangrid and Swipple, are weaving with drawn swords. The shaft shall sing, the shield shall ring, the helm-hound [axe] shall fall on the target.[2]

And those who met their death in battle had reserved for them a similar existence in the life to come, not doomed like the 'straw-dead' to tread wet and chill and dusky ways to the land of Hel, but — I am quoting Gummere [3] — as weapon-dead faring "straightway to Odin, unwasted by sickness, in the full strength of manhood," to spend their days in glorious battle and their nights in equally glorious feasting in the courts of Valhalla.

In his cradle the young Viking was lulled by such songs as this: —

[1] *Corpus Poeticum Boreale*, I, pp. 268–70.     [2] *Ibid.*, I, p. 281 *f.*
[3] *Germanic Origins* (New York, 1892), p. 305 *f.*

My mother said they should buy me a boat and fair oars, and that I should go abroad with the Vikings, should stand forward in the bows and steer a dear bark, and so wend to the haven and cut down man after man there.

When he grows up the earl's daughter scorns him as a boy who "has never given a warm meal to the wolf," "seen the raven in autumn scream over the carrion draft," or "been where the shell-thin edges" of the blades crossed; whereupon he wins a place by her side by replying: —

I have walked with bloody brand and with whistling spear, with the wound-bird following me. The Vikings made a fierce attack; we raised a furious storm, the flame ran over the dwellings of men, we laid the bleeding corses to rest in the gates of the city.[1]

And at the end, like Ragnar Lodbrok captured and dying in the pit of serpents, he can tell his tale of feeding the eagle and the she-wolf since he first reddened the sword at the age of twenty, and end his life undaunted to the ever-recurring refrain, "We hewed with the sword":

Death has no terrors. I am willing to depart. They are calling me home, the Fays whom Woden the Lord of Hosts has sent me from his hall. Merrily shall I drink ale in my high-seat with the Anses. My life days are done. Laughing will I die.[2]

Politically, Viking society was aristocratic, but an aristocracy in which all the nobles were equal. "We have no lord, we are all equal," said Rollo's men when

---

[1] *Corpus Poeticum Boreale*, I, p. 373.     [2] *Ibid.*, II, p. 345.

asked who was their lord; and men thus minded were not likely to spend their time casting dice in King Harold's court, even if their independence meant the wolf's lot of exile. What kind of a political organization they were likely to form can be seen from two examples of the Viking age. One is Iceland, described by Lord Bryce [1] as "an almost unique instance of a community whose culture and creative power flourished independently of any favoring material conditions," — that curiously decentralized and democratic commonwealth where the necessities of life created a government with judicial and legislative duties, while the feeling of equality and local independence prevented the government from acquiring any administrative or executive functions, — a community with "a great deal of law and no central executive, a great many courts and no authority to carry out their judgments." The other example is Jomburg, that strange body of Jomvikings established in Pomerania, at the mouth of the Oder, and held by a military gild under the strictest discipline. Only men of undoubted bravery between the ages of eighteen and fifty were admitted to membership; no women were allowed in the castle, and no man could be absent from it for more than three days at a time. Members assumed the duty of mutual support and revenge, and plunder was to be distributed by lot.

[1] "Primitive Iceland," in his *Studies in History and Jurisprudence* (Oxford, 1901), pp. 263 *ff.*

Neither of these types of Viking community was to be reproduced in Normandy, for both were the outgrowth of peculiar local conditions, and the Northmen were too adaptable to found states with a rubber-stamp. A loose half-state like Iceland could exist only where the absence of neighbors or previous inhabitants removed all danger of complications, whether domestic or foreign. A strict warrior gild like that of Jomburg could arise only in a fortress. Whatever form Viking society would take in Normandy was certain to be determined in large measure by local conditions; yet it might well contain elements found in the other societies — the Icelandic sense of equality and independence, and the military discipline of the Jomvikings set in the midst of their Wendish foes. And both of these elements are characteristic of the Norman state.

Such, very briefly sketched, were the Northmen who came to Normandy. We have now to follow them in their new home.

We must note in the first place that the relations between Normandy and the north were not ended with the grant of 911. We must think of the new Norman state, not as a planet sent off into space to move separate and apart in a new orbit, but as a colony, an outpost of the Scandinavian peoples in the south, fed by new bands of colonists from the northern home and only gradually drawn away from its connections with the north and brought into the political system of

Frankish Gaul and its neighbors. For something like a hundred years after the coming of Rollo the key to Norman history is found in this fact and in the resulting interplay of Scandinavian and Frankish influences. The very grant of 911 was susceptible of being differently regarded from the point of view of the two parties. Charles the Simple probably thought he was creating a new fief with the Norman chief as his vassal, bound to him by feudal ties, while to Rollo, innocent of feudal ideas, the grant may well have seemed a gift outright to be held by himself and his companions as land was held at home. From one point of view a feudal holding, from another an independent Scandinavian state, the contradiction in Normandy's position explains much of its early history. The new colony was saved from absorption in its surroundings by continued migration from the north; before it became Frankish and feudal it thus had time to establish itself firmly and draw tightly the lines which separated it from its neighbors. At once a Frankish county and a Danish colony, it slowly formed itself into the semi-independent duchy which is the historic Normandy of the eleventh and twelfth centuries.

Although Rollo was baptized in 912 and signalized his conversion by extensive grants of land to the great churches and monasteries of his new territories, his Christianity sat lightly upon him and left him a Norse sea-rover at heart till the end, when he sought to appease the powers of the other world, not only by gifts of gold to the church, but by human sacrifices to the northern gods. His legislation, so far as it can be reconstructed from the shadowy accounts of later historians, was fundamentally Scandinavian in character, and his followers guarded jealously the northern traditions of equality and independence. His son, William Longsword, was a more Christian and Frankish type, but his death, celebrated in a Latin poem which represents the earliest known example of popular epic in Normandy, was the signal for a Scandinavian and pagan reaction. We hear of fresh arrivals on the Seine, Vikings who worshipped Thor and Odin, of an independent band at Bayeux under a certain Haigrold or Harold, and even of appeals for reënforcements from the Normans to the Northmen beyond the sea. The dukes of Rouen, says the *Saga of St. Olaf*, "remember well their kinship with the chiefs of Norway; they hold them in such honor that they have always been the best friends of the Norwegians, and all the Norwegians who wish find refuge in Normandy." Not till the beginning of the eleventh century does the Scandinavian immigration come to an end and Normandy stand fully on its own feet.

Not until the eleventh century also does the history of Normandy emerge from the uncertain period of legend and tradition and reach an assured basis of contemporary evidence. Throughout Europe, the tenth century is one of the most uncertain and obscure of all the Christian centuries. To the critic, as an Oxford don distinguished for knowledge of this epoch once remarked, its delightful obscurity makes it all the more interesting, but there are limits to the delights of obscurity, and a French scholar who has tried to reconstruct the history of this period in Spain finds that all surviving documentary sources of information are fabrications! Matters are not so bad as that for Normandy, for the forgers there chose other periods in which to place their products, but there are for the tenth century practically no contemporary documents or contemporary Norman chronicles. The earliest Norman historian, Dudo, dean of Saint-Quentin, wrote after the year 1000 and had no personal knowledge of the beginnings of the Norman state. Diffuse, rhetorical, credulous, and ready to distort events in order to glorify the ancestors of the Norman dukes who were his patrons, Dudo is anything but a trustworthy writer, and only the most circumspect criticism can glean a few facts from his confused and turgid rhetoric. Yet he was copied by his Norman successors, in prose and in verse, and has found his defenders among patriotic Normans of a more modern time. Not until quite recent years has his fundamental untrustworthiness been fully established, and with it has vanished all hope of any detailed knowledge of early Norman history. Only with the eleventh century do we reach a solid foundation of annals and charters in the reigns of the princes whom Dudo seeks to glorify in the person of their predecessors. And when we reach this period, the heroic age of conquest and settlement is over, and the Normans have become much as other Frenchmen.

At this point the fundamental question forces itself upon us, how far was Normandy affected by Scandinavian influences? What in race and language, in law and custom, was the contribution of the north to Normandy? And the answer must be that in most respects the tangible contribution was slight. Whatever may have been the state of affairs in the age of colonization and settlement, by the century which followed the Normans had become to a surprising degree absorbed by their environment.

It is now generally admitted, says Professor Maitland,[1] that for at least half a century before the battle of Hastings, the Normans were Frenchmen, French in their language, French in their law, proud indeed of their past history, very ready to fight against other Frenchmen if Norman home-rule was endangered, but still Frenchmen, who regarded Normandy as a member of the state or congeries of states that owed service, we can hardly say obedience, to the king at Paris. Their spoken language was French, their written language was Latin, but the Latin of France; the style of their legal documents was the style of the French chancery; very few of the technical terms of their law were of Scandinavian origin. When at length the 'custom' of Normandy appears in writing, it takes its place among other French customs, and this although for a long time past Normandy has formed one of the dominions of a prince, between whom and the king of the French there has been little love and

---

[1] Pollock and Maitland, *History of English Law*, I, p. 66.

frequent war; and the peculiar characteristics which mark off the custom of Normandy from other French customs seem due much rather to the legislation of Henry of Anjou than to any Scandinavian tradition.

The law of Normandy was by this time Frankish, and its speech was French. Even the second duke, William Longsword, found it necessary to send his son to Bayeux to learn Norse, for it was no longer spoken at Rouen. And in the French of Normandy, the Norman dialect, the Scandinavian element is astonishingly small, as careful students of the local *patois* tell us. Only in one department of life, the life of the sea, is any considerable Scandinavian influence discernible, and the historian of the French navy, Bourel de la Roncière, has some striking pages on the survivals of the language of the Norse Vikings in the daily speech of the French sailor and fisherman.

The question of race is more difficult, and is of course quite independent of the question of language, for language, as has been well said, is not a test of race but a test of social contact, and the fundamental physical characteristics of race are independent of speech. "Skulls," says Rhys, "are harder than consonants, and races lurk behind when languages slip away." On this point again scientific examination is unfavorable to extended Scandinavian influence. Pronounced northern types, of course, occur, — I remember, on my first journey through Normandy, seeing at a wayside station a peasant who might have walked that moment out of a Wisconsin lumber-camp or a Minnesota wheat-field, — but the statistics of anthropometry show a steady preponderance of the round-headed type which prevails in other parts of France. Only in two regions does the Teutonic type assert itself strongly, in the lower valley of the Seine and in the Cotentin, and it is in these regions and at points along the shore that place-names of Scandinavian origin are most frequent. The terminations *bec* and *fleur*, *beuf* and *ham* and *dalle* and *tot* — Bolbec, Harfleur, Quillebeuf, Ouistreham, Dieppedalle, Yvetot — tell the same story as the terms used in navigation, namely that the Northmen were men of the sea and settled in the estuaries and along the coast. The earlier population, however, though reduced by war and pillage and famine, was not extinguished. It survived in sufficient numbers to impose its language on its conquerors, to preserve throughout the greater part of the country its fundamental racial type, and to make these Northmen of the sea into Normans of the land.

What, then, was the Scandinavian contribution to the making of Normandy if it was neither law nor speech nor race? First and foremost, it was Normandy itself, created as a distinct entity by the Norman occupation and the grant to Rollo and his followers, without whom it would have remained an undifferentiated part of northern France. Next, a new element in the population, numerically small in proportion to the mass, but a leaven to the whole — quick to absorb Frankish law and Christian culture but retaining its northern qualities of enterprise, of daring, and of leadership. It is no accident that the names of the leaders in early Norman movements are largely Norse. And finally a race of princes, high-handed and masterful but with a talent for political organization, state-builders at home and abroad, who made Normandy the strongest and most centralized principality in France and joined to it a kingdom beyond the seas which became the strongest state in western Europe.

## BIBLIOGRAPHICAL NOTE

The best outline of the beginnings of Normandy is H. Prentout, *Essai sur les origines et la fondation du duché de Normandie* (Paris, 1911). For the Frankish side of the Norse expeditions see W. Vogel, *Die Normannen und das fränkische Reich* (Heidelberg, 1906), supplemented by F. Lot, in the *Bibliothèque de l'École des Chartes*, LXIX (1908). Their devastation of Normandy is illustrated by the fate of the monastery of Saint-Wandrille: F. Lot, *Études critiques sur l'abbaye de Saint-Wandrille* (Paris, 1913), ch. 3. There is a vast literature in the Scandinavian languages; for the titles of fundamental works by Steenstrup, Munch, Worsaae, and Alexander Bugge, see Charles Gross, *Sources and Literature of English History* (London, 1915), § 42. Considerable material in English has been published in the *Saga-Book* of the Viking Society (London, since 1895). On the material culture of the north see Sophus Müller, *Nordische Altertumskunde* (Strassburg, 1897–98), and the various works of Montelius. The early poetry is collected and translated by Vigfusson and Powell, *Corpus Poeticum Boreale* (Oxford, 1883). Convenient summaries in English are C. F. Keary, *The Vikings in Western Christendom* (London, 1891); A. Mawer, *The Vikings* (Cambridge, 1913); and L. M. Larson, *Canute the Great* (New York, 1912).

# III

## NORMANDY AND ENGLAND

A FTER the coming of the Northmen the chief event in Norman history is the conquest of England, and just as relations with the north are the chief feature of the tenth century, so relations with England dominate the eleventh century, and the central point is the conquest of 1066. In this series of events the central figure is, of course, William the Conqueror, by descent duke of Normandy and by conquest king of England.

Of William's antecedents we have no time to speak at length. Grandson of the fourth Norman duke, Richard the Good, William was the son of Duke Robert, who met his death in Asia Minor in 1035 while returning from a pilgrimage to Jerusalem. To distinguish him from the later duke of the same name he is called Robert I or Robert the Magnificent, sometimes and quite incorrectly, Robert the Devil, by an unwarranted confusion with this hero, or rather villain, of romance and grand opera. A contemporary of the great English king Canute, Robert was a man of renown in the Europe of the early eleventh century, and if our sources of information permitted us to know the history of his brief reign, we should probably find that much that was distinctive of the Normandy of his son's day can be traced back to his time. More than once in history has a great father been eclipsed by a greater son. The fact should be added, which William's contemporaries never allowed him to forget, that he was an illegitimate son. His mother Arlette was the daughter of a tanner of Falaise, and while it is not clear that Duke Robert was ever married to any one else, his union with Arlette had no higher sanction than the Danish custom of his forefathers. Their son was generally known in his day as William the Bastard, and only the great achievements of his reign succeeded in replacing this, first by William the Great and later by William the Conqueror.

Were it not for the resulting confusion with other great Williams, — one of whom has recently been raised by admiring subjects to the rank of William the Greatest! — there would be a certain advantage in retaining the title of great, in order to remind ourselves that William was not only a conqueror but a great ruler. The greatest secular figure in the Europe of his day, he is also one of the greatest in the line of English sovereigns, whether we judge him by capacity for rule or by the results of his reign, and none has had a more profound effect on the whole current of English history. The late Edward A. Freeman, who devoted five stout volumes to the history of the Norman Conquest and of William, and who never shrank from superlatives, goes still further:—

No man that ever trod this earth was ever endowed with greater natural gifts; to no man was it ever granted to accomplish greater things. If we look only to the scale of a man's acts without regard to their moral character, we must hail in the victor of Val-ès-dunes, of Varaville, and of Senlac, in the restorer of Normandy, the Conqueror of England, one who may fairly claim his place in the first rank of the world's greatest men. No man ever did his work more thoroughly at the moment; no man ever left his work behind him as more truly an abiding possession for all time. . . . If we cannot give him a niche among pure patriots and heroes, he is quite as little entitled to a place among mere tyrants and destroyers. William of Normandy has no claim to a share in the pure glory of Timoleon, Ælfred, and Washington; he cannot even claim the more mingled fame of Alexander, Charles, and Cnut; but he has still less in common with the mere enemies of their species, with the Nabuchodonosors, the Swegens, and the Buonapartes, whom God has sent from time to time as simple scourges of a guilty world. . . . He never wholly cast away the thoughts of justice and mercy, and in his darkest hours had still somewhat of the fear of God before his eyes.[1]

I have quoted the essence of Freeman's characterization, not because it seems to me wholly just or even historical, but in order to set forth vividly the importance of William and his work. It is not the historian's business to award niches in a hall of fame. He is no Rhadamanthus, to separate the Alfreds of this world from the Nebuchadnezzars, the Washingtons from the Napoleons. So far as he deals with individuals, his business is to explain to us each man in the light of his time

[1] *History of the Norman Conquest* (third edition), II, pp. 164-67.

and its conditions, not to compare him with men of far distant times and places in order to arrange all in a final scale of values. It was once the fashion in debating societies to discuss whether Demosthenes was a greater orator than Cicero, and whether either was the equal of Daniel Webster. It is even more futile to consider whether William the Conqueror was a greater man than Alexander or a less than George Washington, for the quantities are incommensurable. So far as comparisons of this sort are at all legitimate, they must be instituted between similar things, between contemporaries or between men in quick sequence. When they deal with wide intervals of time and circumstance, they wrest each man from his true setting and become fundamentally unhistorical.

An able general, strong in battle and still stronger in strategy and craft, a skilful diplomat, a born ruler of men, William was yet greater in the combination of vision, patience, and masterful will which make the statesman, and the results of his statesmanship are writ large on the page of English history. To his contemporaries his most striking characteristic was his pitiless strength and inflexible will, and if they had been familiar with Nietzsche's theory of the 'overman,' they would certainly have placed him in that class. Stark and stern and wrathful, the author of the Anglo-Saxon *Chronicle* approaches him, as Freeman well says,[1] "with

---

[1] *Norman Conquest*, II, p. 166.

downcast eyes and bated breath, as if he were hardly dealing with a man of like passions with himself but were rather drawing the portrait of a being of another nature." This, the most adequate characterization of the *Uebermensch* of the eleventh century, runs as follows: [1]

If any would know what manner of man king William was, the glory that he obtained, and of how many lands he was lord; then will we describe him as we have known him, we, who have looked upon him and who once lived in his court. This king William, of whom we are speaking, was a very wise and a great man, and more honoured and more powerful than any of his predecessors. He was mild to those good men who loved God, but severe beyond measure towards those who withstood his will. He founded a noble monastery on the spot where God permitted him to conquer England, and he established monks in it, and he made it very rich. In his days the great monastery at Canterbury was built, and many others also throughout England; moreover this land was filled with monks who lived after the rule of St. Benedict; and such was the state of religion in his days that all that would might observe that which was prescribed by their respective orders. King William was also held in much reverence: he wore his crown three times every year when he was in England: at Easter he wore it at Winchester, at Pentecost at Westminster, and at Christmas at Gloucester. And at these times, all the men of England were with him, archbishops, bishops, abbots, and earls, thanes, and knights. So also, was he a very stern and a wrathful man, so that none durst do anything against his will, and he kept in prison those earls who acted against his pleasure. He removed bishops from their sees, and abbots from their offices, and

[1] Translated by Giles (London, 1847), pp. 461–63.

he imprisoned thanes, and at length he spared not his own brother Odo. This Odo was a very powerful bishop in Normandy, his see was that of Bayeux, and he was foremost to serve the king. He had an earldom in England, and when William was in Normandy he was the first man in this country, and him did he cast into prison. Amongst other things the good order that William established is not to be forgotten; it was such that any man, who was himself aught, might travel over the kingdom with a bosom-full of gold unmolested; and no man durst kill another, however great the injury he might have received from him. He reigned over England, and being sharp-sighted to his own interest, he surveyed the kingdom so thoroughly that there was not a single hide of land throughout the whole of which he knew not the possessor, and how much it was worth, and this he afterwards entered in his register. The land of the Britons was under his sway, and he built castles therein; moreover he had full dominion over the Isle of Man [Anglesey]: Scotland also was subject to him from his great strength; the land of Normandy was his by inheritance, and he possessed the earldom of Maine; and had he lived two years longer he would have subdued Ireland by his prowess, and that without a battle. Truly there was much trouble in these times, and very great distress; he caused castles to be built, and oppressed the poor. The king was also of great sternness, and he took from his subjects many marks of gold, and many hundred pounds of silver, and this, either with or without right, and with little need. He was given to avarice, and greedily loved gain. He made large forests for the deer, and enacted laws therewith, so that whoever killed a hart or a hind should be blinded. As he forbade killing the deer, so also the boars; and he loved the tall stags as if he were their father. He also appointed concerning the hares, that they should go free. The rich complained and the poor murmured, but he was so sturdy that he recked nought of them; they must will all that the king willed, if they would live; or would keep their lands; or would hold their possessions; or would be maintained in their rights. Alas! that any man should so exalt himself, and carry himself in his pride over all! May Almighty God show mercy to his soul, and grant him the forgiveness of his sins! We have written concerning him these things, both good and bad, that virtuous men might follow after the good, and wholly avoid the evil, and might go in the way that leadeth to the kingdom of heaven.

This *Requiescat* of the monk of Peterborough has carried us forward half a century, till the Conqueror, in the full maturity of his power and strength, rode to his death down the steep street of the burning town of Mantes and was buried in his own great abbey-church at Caen. And the good peace that he gave the land at the end came, both in Normandy and in England, only after many stormy years of war, rebellion, and strife. William was but sixty when he died; when his father was laid away in the basilica of far-off Nicæa, he was only seven or at most eight. The conquest of England was made in his fortieth year, when he had already reigned thirty-one years as duke. Or, if we deduct the years of his youth, the conquest of England falls just halfway between his coming of age and his death. I give these figures to adjust the perspective. William's place in the line of English kings is so prominent and his achievements in England are so important that they always tend to overshadow in our minds his earlier years as duke. Yet without these formative years there could have been no conquest of England, and without some study of them that conquest cannot be understood.

If we pass over rapidly, as for lack of information we must needs do, the dozen years of William's minority, we find his reign in Normandy chiefly occupied with his struggles with his vassals, his neighbors, and the king of France, all a necessary consequence of his feudal position as duke.   The Norman vassals, always turbulent and rebellious, seem to have broken forth anew upon the death of Robert the Magnificent, and such accounts as have reached us of the events of the next twelve years reveal a constant state of anarchy and disorder.   The revolt of the barons came to a head in 1047, when the whole of Lower Normandy rose under the leadership of the two chief *vicomtes* of the region, Ranulf of Bayeux and Néel of Saint-Sauveur, the ruins of whose family castle of Saint-Sauveur-le-Vicomte still greet the traveller who leaves Cherbourg for Paris.   William, who was hunting in the neighborhood of Valognes, was obliged to flee half-clad in the night and to pick his way alone by devious paths across the enemy's country to his castle of Falaise.   With the assistance of the French king he was able to collect an army from Upper Normandy and meet the rebels on the great plain of Val-des-Dunes, near Caen, where the *Mont-joie* of the French and the *Dex aie* of the duke's followers answered the barons' appeals to their local saints of St. Sauveur, St. Sever, and St. Amand.   William was victorious; the leaders of the revolt were sent into exile, but one of them, Grimoud of Plessis, the traitor, apparently he who had sought William's death in the night at Valognes, was put in prison at Rouen in irons which he wore until his death.

With the collapse of the great revolt and the razing of the castles of the revolting barons, Normandy began to enjoy a period of internal peace and order. Externally, however, difficulties rather increased with the growing power of the young duke. In discussions of feudal society it is too often assumed that if the feudal obligations are observed between lords and vassals, all will go well, and that the anarchy of which the Middle Ages are full was the result of violations of these feudal ties. Now, while undoubtedly a heavy account must be laid at the door of direct breaches of the feudal bond, it must also be remembered that there was a fundamental defect in the very structure of feudal society. We may express this defect by saying that the feudal ties were only vertical and not lateral. The lord was bound to his vassal and the vassal to his lord, and so far as these relations went they provided a nexus of social and legal relations which might hold society together. But there was no tie between two vassals of the same lord, nothing whatever which bound one of them to live in peace and amity with the other. Quite the contrary. War being the normal state of European society in the feudal period, the right to carry on private war was one of the cherished rights of the feudal baron, and it extended wherever it was not restricted by the bonds of fealty and vassalage. The duke of Normandy and the count of Anjou were both vassals of the king of France, but their relations to each other were those of complete independence, and, save for some special agreement or friendship, were normally relations of hostility.

And so an important part of Norman history has to treat of the struggles with the duchy's neighbors, Flanders on the north, the royal domain on the east, Maine and Anjou to the southward, and Brittany on the west. Fortunately for Normandy, the Bretons were but loosely organized, while the Flemings, compacted into one of the strongest of the French fiefs, were generally friendly, and the friendship was in this period cemented by William's marriage to Matilda, daughter of the count of Flanders, one of the few princely marriages of the time which was founded upon affection and observed with fidelity. With Anjou the case was different. Beginning as a border county over against the Bretons of the lower Loire, with the black rock of Angers as its centre and fortress, Anjou, though still comparatively small in area, had grown into one of the strongest states of western France. Under a remarkable line of counts, Geoffrey Greygown, Fulk the Red, and Fulk the Black, ancestors of the Plantagenet kings of England, it had become the dominant power on the Loire, and now under their successor Geoffrey the Hammer it threatened further expansion by hammering its frontiers still further to the north and east. Geoffrey, William's contemporary and rival, is known to us by a striking characterization written by his nephew and successor and forming a typical bit of feudal biography: [1]

My uncle Geoffrey became a knight in his father's lifetime and began his knighthood by wars against his neighbors, one against the Poitevins, whose count he captured at Mont Couër, and another against the people of Maine, whose count, named Herbert Bacon, he likewise took. He also carried on war against his own father, in the course of which he committed many evil deeds of which he afterward bitterly repented. After his father died on his return from Jerusalem, Geoffrey possessed his lands and the city of Angers, and fought Count Thibaud of Blois, son of Count Odo, and by gift of King Henry received the city of Tours, which led to another war with Count Thibaud, in the course of which, at a battle between Tours and Amboise, Thibaud was captured with a thousand of his knights. And so, besides the part of Touraine inherited from his father, he acquired Tours and the castles round about — Chinon, L'Ile-Bouchard, Châteaurenault, and Saint-Aignan. After this he had a war with William, count of the Normans, who later acquired the kingdom of England and was a magnificent king, and with the people of France and of Bourges, and with William count of Poitou and Aimeri viscount of Thouars and Hoel count of Nantes and the Breton counts of Rennes and with Hugh count of Maine, who had thrown off his fealty. Because of all these wars and the prowess he showed therein he was rightly called the Hammer, as one who hammered down his enemies.

[1] Fulk Rechin, in *Chroniques des comtes d'Anjou* (ed. Marchegay), p. 378 f; (ed. Halphen and Poupardin, Paris, 1913), pp. 235-37.

In the last year of his life he made me his nephew a knight at the age of seventeen in the city of Angers, at the feast of Pentecost, in the year of the Incarnation 1060, and granted me Saintonge and the city of Saintes because of a quarrel he had with Peter of Didonne. In this same year King Henry died on the nativity of St. John, and my uncle Geoffrey on the third day after Martinmas came to a good end. For in the night which preceded his death, laying aside all care of knighthood and secular things, he became a monk in the monastery of St. Nicholas, which his father and he had built with much devotion and endowed with their goods.

The great source of conflict between William and Geoffrey was the intervening county of Maine, whence the Angevins had gained possession of the Norman fortresses of Domfront and Alençon, and it was not till after Geoffrey's death, in 1063, that the capture of its chief city, LeMans, completed that union of Normandy and Maine which was to last through the greater part of Norman history. The conquest of Maine was the first fruit of William's work as conqueror.

With William's suzerain, the king of France, relations were more complicated. Legally there could be no question that the duke of Normandy was the feudal vassal of the French king and as such bound to the obligations of loyalty and service which flowed from his oath of homage and fealty. Actually, in the society of the eleventh and twelfth centuries, such bonds were freely and frequently broken, yet they were not thrown off. Here, as in many other phases of mediæval life, we meet that persistent contradiction between theory and practice which shocks our more consistent minds. Just as the men of the Middle Ages tolerated a Holy Roman Empire which claimed universal dominion and often exercised only the most local and rudimentary authority, so they accepted a monarchy like that of the early Capetians, which claimed to rule over the whole of France and was limited in its actual government to a few farms and castles in the neighborhood of Paris. And just as they maintained ideals of lofty chivalry and rigorous asceticism far beyond the sordid reality of ordinary knighthood or monkhood, so the constant violation of feudal obligations did not change the feudal bond or destroy the nexus of feudal relations. In this age of unrestraint, ferocious savagery alternated with knightly generosity, and ungovernable rage with self-abasing penance.

At such times the relations of the king and his great feudatories would depend very largely upon personal temperament, political situations, and even the impulse of the moment, and we must not expect to find such purpose and continuity in policies as prevail in more settled periods. Nevertheless, with due allowance for momentary variations, the relations of Normandy with the Capetian kings follow comparatively simple lines. The position of Normandy in the Seine valley and its proximity to the royal domain offered endless opportunity for friction, yet for about a century strained relations were avoided by alliance and friendship based upon common interest. Hugh Capet came to the throne with the support of the Norman duke, and his successors often found their mainstay in Norman arms. Robert the Magnificent on his departure for the East commended his young son to King Henry, and the heir seems to have grown up under the king's guardianship. It was Henry who saved William from his barons in 1047, and it was William that furnished over half the king's soldiers on the campaign against Anjou in the following year. Then, about the middle of the eleventh century, comes a change, for which the growing power and influence of Normandy furnish a sufficient explanation. Henry supported the revolt of William of Arques in 1053 and attempted a great invasion of Normandy in the same year, while in 1058 he burnt and pillaged his way into the heart of the Norman territory. A waiting game and well-timed attacks defeated these efforts at Mortemer and at Varaville, but William refused to follow up his advantage by a direct attack upon his king, whom he continued to treat with personal consideration as his feudal lord. Even after William himself became king, he seems to have continued to render the military service which he owed as duke. By this time, however, the subjection had become only nominal; merely as duke, William was now a more powerful ruler than the king of France, and the Capetian monarchy had to bide its time for more than a century longer.

Before we can leave the purely Norman period of William's reign and turn to the conquest of England, it is important to examine the internal condition of Normandy under his rule. Even the most thorough study possible of this subject would need to be brief, for lack of available evidence. Time has not dealt kindly with Norman records, and over against the large body of Anglo-Saxon charters and the unique account of Anglo-Saxon England preserved in the Domesday survey, contemporary Normandy can set only a few scattered documents and a curious statement of the duke's rights and privileges under William, drawn up four years after his death and only recently recovered as an authority for his reign. The sources of Norman history were probably never so abundant as those of England; certainly there is now nothing on the Continent, outside of the Vatican, that can compare with the extraordinarily full and continuous series of the English public records. The great gaps in the Norman records, often supposed to be due to the Revolution, really appear much earlier. Undoubtedly there was in many places wanton destruction of documents in the revolutionary uprisings, and there were many losses under the primitive organization of local archives in this period, as there undoubtedly were during the carelessness and corruption of the Restoration. Nevertheless, an examination of the copies and extracts made from monastic and cathedral archives by the scholars of the seventeenth and eighteenth centuries shows that, with a few significant exceptions, the materials for early Norman history were little richer then than now, so that the great losses must have occurred before this time, that is to say, during the Middle Ages and in the devastation of the English invasion and of the Protestant wars of the sixteenth century. The cathedral library at Bayeux, for example, possesses three volumes of a huge cartulary charred by the fire into which it was thrown when the town was sacked by the Protestants. On the other hand, it should be noted that the French Revolution accomplished one beneficent result for local records in the secularization of ecclesiastical archives and their collection into the great repositories of the Archives Départementales, whose organization is still the envy of historical scholars across the Channel. One who has enjoyed for many months access to these admirable collections of records will be permitted to express his gratitude to those who created them, as well as to those by whom they are now so courteously administered.

Piecing together our scattered information regarding the Normandy of the eleventh century, we note at the outset that it was a feudal society, that is to say, land was for the most part held of a lord by hereditary tenure on condition of military service. Indeed feudal ideas had spread so far that they even penetrated the church, so that in some instances the revenues of the clergy had been granted to laymen and archdeaconries and prebends had been turned into hereditary fiefs. With feudal service went the various incidents of feudal tenure and a well-developed feudal jurisdiction of the lord over his tenants and of the greater barons over the less. In all this there is nothing to distinguish Normandy from the neighboring countries of northern France, and as a feudal society is normally a decentralized society, we should expect to find the powers of government chiefly in the hands of the local lords. A closer study, however, shows certain peculiarities which are of the utmost importance, both for Norman and for English history.

First of all, the military service owing to the duke had been systematically assessed in rough units of five or ten knights, and this service, or its subdivisions, had become attached to certain pieces of land, or knights' fees. The amounts of service were fixed by custom and were regularly enforced. Still more significant are the restrictions placed upon the military power of the barons. The symbol and the foundation of feudal authority was the castle, wherefore the duke forbade the building of castles and strongholds without his license and required them to be handed over to him on demand. Private war and the blood feud could not yet be prohibited entirely, but they were closely limited. No one was allowed to go out to seek his enemy with hauberk and standard and sounding horn. Assaults and ambushes were not permitted in the duke's forests; captives were not to be taken in a feud, nor could arms, horses, or property be carried off from a combat. Burning, plunder, and waste were forbidden in pursuing claims to land, and except for open crime, no one could be condemned to loss of limb unless by judgment of the proper ducal or baronial court. Coinage, generally a valued privilege of the greater lords, was in Normandy a monopoly of the duke. What the absence of such restrictions might mean is well illustrated in England in the reign of Stephen, when private war, unlicensed castles, and baronial coinage appeared as the chief evils of an unbridled feudal anarchy.

In the administration of justice, in spite of the great franchises of the barons, the duke has a large reserved jurisdiction. Certain places are under his special protection, certain crimes put the offender at his mercy. The administrative machinery, though in many respects still primitive, has kept pace with the duke's authority. Whereas the Capetian king has as his local representatives only the semi-feudal agents on his farms, the Norman duke has for purposes of local government a real public officer, the *vicomte*, commanding his troops, guarding his castles, maintaining order, administering justice, and collecting the ducal revenues. Nowhere is the superiority of the Norman dukes over their royal overlords more clear than in the matter of finance. The housekeeping of the Capetian king of the eleventh century was still what the Germans call a *Naturalwirthschaft*, an economic organization based upon payment in produce and labor rather than in money. "Less powerful than certain of his great vassals," as he is described by his principal historian, Luchaire,[1] "the king lives like them from the income from his farms and tolls, the payments of his peasants, the labor of his serfs, the taxes disguised as gifts which he levies from the bishops and abbots of the neighborhood. His granaries of Gonesse, Janville, Mantes, Étampes, furnish his grain; his cellars of Orleans and Argenteuil, his wine; his forests of Rouvrai (now the Bois de Boulogne), Saint-Germain, Fontainebleau, Iveline, Compiègne, his game. He passes his time in hunting, for amusement or to supply his table, and travels constantly from estate to estate, from abbey to abbey, obliged to make full use of his rights of entertainment and to move frequently from place to place in order not to exhaust the resources of his subjects."

In other words, under existing methods of communication, it was easier to transport the king and his household than it was to transport food, and the king literally 'boarded round' from farm to farm. Such conditions were typical of the age, and they could only be changed by the development of a revenue in money, enabling the king to buy where he would and to pay whom he would for service, whether personal or political or military. Only by hard cash could the mediæval ruler become

---

[1] Luchaire, *Les quatre premiers Capétiens*, in Lavisse, *Histoire de France* (Paris, 1901), II, 2, p. 176.

independent of the limitations which feudalism placed upon him. Now, while the Norman duke derived much of his income from his farms and forests, his mills and fishing rights and local monopolies and tolls, he had also a considerable revenue in money. Each *vicomté* was farmed for a fixed amount, and there was probably a regular method of collection and accounting. If the king wished to bestow revenue upon a monastery he would grant so many measures of grain at the mills of Bourges or so many measures of wine in the vineyards of Joui; while in a similar position the Norman duke would give money — twelve pounds in the farm of Argentan, sixty shillings and tenpence in the toll of Exmes, or one hundred shillings in the *prévôté* of Caen. Nothing could show more clearly the superiority of Normandy in fiscal and hence in political organization, where under the forms of feudalism we can already discern the beginnings of the modern state.

To William's authority in the state we must add his control over the Norman church. Profoundly secularized and almost absorbed into the lay society about it as a result of the Norse invasion, the Norman church had been renewed and refreshed by the wave of monastic reform which swept over western Europe in the first half of the eleventh century, and now occupied both spiritually and intellectually a position of honor and of strength. But it was not supreme. The duke appointed its bishops and most of its abbots, sat in its provincial councils, and revised the judgments of its courts. Liberal in gifts to the church and punctilious in his religious observances, William left no doubt who was master, and his respectful but independent attitude toward the Papacy already foreshadowed the conflict in which he forced even the mighty Hildebrand to yield.

I have dwelt at some length upon these matters of internal organization, not only because they are fundamental to an understanding of many institutions of the Norman empire, but because they also serve to explain how there came to be a Norman empire. The conquest of England has been so uniformly approached from the English point of view that it is often made to appear as more or less of an accident arising from a casual invasion of freebooters. Viewed in its proper perspective, which I venture to think is the Norman perspective, it appears as a natural outgrowth of Norman discipline and of Norman expansion. Only because the duke was strong at home could he hope to be strong abroad, only because he was master of an extraordinarily vigorous, coherent, and well-organized state in Normandy could he attempt the at first sight impossible task of conquering a kingdom and the still greater task of organizing it under a firm government. We must take account, not only of the weakness of England, but also of the strength of Normandy, stronger than any of its continental neighbors, stronger even than royalty itself.

That the expansion of Normandy should be directed toward England was the result, not only of the special conditions of the year 1066, but of a steady *rapprochement* between the two countries, in which the active effort was exerted from the Norman side. By geographical position, by the Scandinavian settlement of both countries, and by the commercial enterprise of the merchants of Rouen, the history of Normandy and England had in various ways been brought together in the tenth century, till in 1002 the marriage of the English king Ethelred with Emma, sister of Duke Richard the Good, created dynastic connections of far-reaching importance. Their son Edward the Confessor was brought up at the Norman court, so that his habits and sympathies became Norman rather than English, and his accession to the English throne in 1042 opened the way to a rapid development of Norman influence both in church and in state, which Freeman, with his strong anti-foreign feelings, considered the real beginning of the Norman Conquest. As Edward's childless reign drew near its end, there were two principal claimants for the succession, Harold, son of Godwin, the most powerful earl of England, and Duke William. Harold could make no hereditary claim to the throne, nor until the eve of Edward's death does he seem to have had the king's support, but he was a man of strength and force and was clearly the leading man of the kingdom. William, as the great-nephew of Ethelred and Emma, was cousin (first cousin once removed) of Edward, a claim which he strengthened by an early expression of Edward in his favor and by an oath which he had exacted from Harold to support his candidacy. The exact facts are not known regarding Harold's oath, made during an involuntary visit to Normandy two or three years before, but it enabled William to pose as the defender of a broken obligation and gave him the great moral advantage of the support of Pope Alexander II, to whom he had the question submitted. At Edward's death Harold had himself chosen by the *witan*, or national council, and crowned, so that he had on his side whatever could come from such legal forms and from the support which lay behind them. We must not, however, commit the anachronism of thinking that he was a national hero or even the candidate of a national party. There was in the eleventh century no such thing as a nation in the sense that the term is understood in the modern world, and the word could least of all be applied to England, broken, divided, and harried by Danish invasions and by internal disunion. Even the notion of the foreigner was still dim and inchoate, and the reign of Canute, to cite no others, had shown England that she had nothing to fear from a king of foreign birth. The contest between Harold, who was half-Danish in blood, and William, big as it was in national consequences, cannot be elevated to the rank of a national struggle.

From the death of Edward the Confessor and the coronation of Harold, in January, 1066, until the crossing of the Channel in September, William was busy with preparations for the invasion of England. Such an expedition transcended the obligation of military service which could be demanded from his feudal vassals, and William was obliged to make a strong appeal to the Norman love of adventure and feats of arms and to promise wide lands and rich booty from his future conquests. He also found it necessary to enlist knights from other parts of France — Brittany, Flanders, Poitou, even adventurers from distant Spain and Sicily. And then there was the question of transport, for Normandy had no fleet and it was no small matter to create in six months the seven hundred boats which William's kinsmen and vassals obligated themselves to provide. All were ready by the end of August at the mouth of the Dives, — as the quaint Hôtel Guillaume-le-Conquérant reminds the American visitor, — but mediæval sailors could not tack against the wind, and six weeks were passed in waiting for a favoring breeze. Finally it was decided to take advantage of a west wind as far as the mouth of the Somme, and here at Saint-Valéry the fleet assembled for the final crossing. Late in September the Normans landed on the beach at Pevensey and marched to Hastings, where, October 15, they met the troops of Harold, fresh from their great victory over the men of Norway at Stamfordbridge.

Few battles of the Middle Ages were of importance equal to that of Hastings, and few are better known. Besides the prose accounts of the Latin chroniclers, we have the contemporary elegiacs of Guy of Amiens and Baudri of Bourgueil, the spirited verse of the *Roman de Rou* of Master Wace, the most detailed narrative but written, unfortunately, a century after the event, and the unique and vivid portrayal of the Bayeux Tapestry. This remarkable monument, which is accessible to all in a variety of editions, consists of a roll of cloth two hundred and thirty feet long and twenty inches in breadth, embroidered in colors with a series of seventy-nine scenes which narrate the history of the Conquest from the departure of Harold on the ill-fated journey which led him to William's court down to the final discomfiture of the English army on the field of Hastings. The episodes, which are designated by brief titles, are well chosen and are executed with a realism of detail which is of the greatest importance for the life and culture of the age. Preserved in the cathedral and later in the municipal Museum of Bayeux — save for a notable interval in 1804, when Napoleon had it exhibited in Paris to arouse enthusiasm for a new French conquest of England, — the tapestry appears from internal evidence to have been originally executed as an ornament for this cathedral by English workmen at the command of Bishop Odo, half-brother of the Conqueror. There is no basis for the common belief that it was the work of Queen Matilda or her ladies, but efforts to place it one or even two centuries later have proved unavailing against the evidence of armor and costume, and the general opinion of scholars now regards it as belonging to the eleventh century and thus substantially contemporary with the events which it depicts.

The modern literature of the battle is also commensurate with its importance. The classic account is found in the third volume of Freeman's majestic *History of the Norman Conquest*, where the story is told with a rare combination of minute detail and spirited narrative which reminds us, it has been said, of a battle of the *Iliad* or a Norse saga. Splendid as this narrative is, its enthusiasm often carries it beyond the evidence of the sources, and in several fundamental points it can no longer be accepted as historically sound. The theory of the palisade upon which Freeman's conception of the English tactics rested has been destroyed by the trenchant criticism of that profound student of Anglo-Norman history, J. Horace Round, and his whole treatment has been vigorously attacked from the point of view of the scientific study of military history by Wilhelm Spatz and his distinguished master, Hans Delbrück, of Berlin. Unfortunately the Berlin critics are influenced too much by certain theories of military organization; they do not call the English soldier of the period a degenerate, but they consider him, and the Norman knight as well, incapable of the disciplined and united action required by all real strategy, incapable even of forming the shield-wall and executing the feigned flight described by the contemporary chroniclers of the battle. While it is true that mediæval fighting was far more individualistic than that of ancient or modern armies and lacked also the flexible conditions which lie at the basis of modern tactics, there is the best of contemporary evidence for a certain amount of strategical movement at Hastings. On one point, however, the modern military critics have compelled us to modify our ideas of the battles of earlier times, namely, with respect to the numbers engaged. Against the constant tendency to magnify the size of the military forces, a tendency accentuated in the Middle Ages by the complete recklessness of chroniclers when dealing with large figures, modern criticism has pointed out the limitations of battle-space, transportation, and commissariat. The five millions with which Xerxes is said to have invaded Greece are a physical impossibility, for Delbrück has shown that, with this number moving under normal conditions, the rear-guard could not have crossed the Tigris when the first Persians reached Thermopylæ. Similarly the fifty or sixty thousand knights attributed to William the Conqueror shrink to one-tenth the number when brought to face with the official lists of English and Norman knights' fees. If William's army did not exceed five or six thousand, that of Harold could not have been much greater and may well have been less; though William's panegyrist places the number of English at 1,200,000, not more than 12,000 could have stood, in the closest formation, on the hill which they occupied at Hastings. Small skirmishes these, to those who have followed the battles of the Marne, the Aisne, the Vistula, and the San, yet none the less important in the world's history!

In spite of all the controversy, the main lines of the battle seem fairly clear. The troops of Harold occupied a well-defended hill eight miles inland from Hastings on the London road, the professional guard of housecarles in front, protected by the solid wall of their shields and supported by the thegns and other fully armed troops, the levies of the countryside behind or at the sides, armed with javelins, stone clubs, and farmers' weapons. They had few archers and no cavalry, but the steep hill was well protected from the assaults of the Norman horse and favored the firm defence which the English tactics dictated. The Norman lines consisted first of archers, then of heavy-armed foot-soldiers, and finally of the mailed horsemen, their centre grouped about William and the standard which he had received from the Pope. After a preliminary attack by the archers and foot, the knights came forward, preceded by the minstrel Taille-fer, "a jongleur whom a very brave heart ennobled," *qui mult bien chantout*, throwing his sword in the air and catching it as he sang —

| | |
|---|---|
| De Karlemaigne e de Rollant | Of Roland and of Charlemagne, |
| E d'Oliver e des vassals | Oliver and the vassals all |
| Qui morurent en Rencevals. | Who fell in fight at Roncevals. |

But the horses recoiled from the hill, pursued by many of the English, and only the sight of William, his head bared of its helmet so as to be seen by his men, rallied the knights again. The mass of the English stood firm behind their shield-wall and their line could be broken only by the ruse of a feigned flight, from which the Normans turned to surround and cut to pieces their pursuers. Even then the housecarles were unmoved, until the arrows of the high-shooting Norman bowmen finally opened up the gaps in their ranks into which William's horsemen pressed against the battle-axes of the king's guard. And then, as darkness began to fall, Harold was mortally wounded by an arrow, the guard was cut to pieces, and the remnant fled. "Here Harold was killed and the English turned to flight" is the final heading in the Bayeux Tapestry, while in the margin the spoilers strip the coats of mail from the dead and drive off the horses of the slain knights.

"A single battle settled the fate of England." There was still grim work to be done — the humbling of Exeter, the harrying of Northumberland, the subjection of the earls, but these were only local episodes. There was no one but William who could effectively take Harold's place, and when on Christmas Day he had been crowned at London, he could reduce opposition at his leisure. The chronicle of these later years belongs to English rather than to Norman history.

The results of the Conquest, too, are of chief significance for the conquered. For the Normans the immediate effect was a great opportunity for expansion in every department of life. There was work for the warrior in completing the subjugation of the land, for the organizer and statesman in the new adjustments of central and local government, for the prelate in bringing his new diocese into line with the practice of the church on the Continent, for the monks to found new priories and administer the new lands which their monasteries now received beyond the Channel. The Norman townsman and the Norman merchant followed hard upon the Norman armies, in the Norman colony in London, in the traders of the ports, in the boroughs of the western border. In part, of course, the change was simply the replacing of one set of persons by another, putting a Norman archbishop in place of Stigand at Canterbury, spreading over the map the Montgomeries and Percies, the Mowbrays and the Mortimers and scores of other household names of English history; but it was also a work of readjustment and reorganization which required all the Norman gift for constructive work. A certain *élan* passes through Norman life and reflects itself in Norman literature, as the Normans become more conscious of the glory of their achievements and the greatness of their new empire. England had become an appendage to Normandy, and men did not yet see that the relation would soon be reversed.

For England, the Norman Conquest determined permanently the orientation of English politics and English culture. Geographically belonging, with the Scandinavian countries, to the outlying lands of Europe, the British Isles had been in serious danger of sharing their remoteness from the general movements of European life and drifting into the back waters of history. The union with Normandy turned England southward and brought it at once into the full current of European affairs — political entanglements, ecclesiastical connections, cultural influences. England became a part of France and thus entered fully into the life of the world to which France belonged. It received the speech of France, the literature of France, and the art of France; its law became in large measure Frankish, its institutions more completely feudal. Yet the connection with France ran through Normandy, and the French influence took on Norman forms. Most of all was this true in the field in which the Norman excelled, that of government: English feudalism was Norman feudalism, in which the barons were weak and the central power strong, and it was the heavy hand of Norman kingship that turned the loose and disintegrating Anglo-Saxon state into the English nation. England was Europeanized only at the price of being Normanized.

From the point of view both of immediate achievement and of ultimate results, the conquest of England was the crowning act of Norman history. Something doubtless was due to good fortune, — to the absence of an English fleet, to the favorable opportunity in French politics, to the mistakes of the English. But the fundamental facts, without which these would have meant nothing, were the strength and discipline of Normandy and the personality of her leader. Diplomat, warrior, leader of men, William was preëminently a statesman, and it was his organizing genius which "turned the defeat of English arms into the making of the English nation." This talent for political organization was, however, no isolated endowment of the Norman duke, but was shared in large measure by the Norman barons, as is abundantly shown by the history of Norman rule in Italy and Sicily. For William and for his followers the conquest of England only gave a wider field for qualities of state-building which had already shown themselves in Normandy.

## BIBLIOGRAPHICAL NOTE

A detailed narrative of the relations between Normandy and England in the eleventh century is given by E. A. Freeman in his *History of the Norman Conquest* (Oxford, 1870–79), but large portions of this work need to be rewritten in the light of later studies, especially those of Round. There is a brief biography of William the Conqueror by Freeman in the series of "Twelve English Statesmen" (London, 1888), and a fuller one by F. M. Stenton in the "Heroes of the Nations" (1908). For the institutions of Normandy see my articles on

"Knight Service in Normandy in the Eleventh Century," in *English Historical Review*, XXII, pp. 636–49; "The Norman 'Consuetudines et Iusticie' of William the Conqueror," *ibid.* XXIII, pp. 502–08; and "Normandy under William the Conqueror," in *American Historical Review*, XIV, pp. 453–76 (1909); also L. Valin, *Le duc de Normandie et sa cour, 912–1204* (Paris, 1910). For church and state, see H. Böhmer, *Kirche und Staat in England und in der Normandie* (Leipzig, 1899). The dealings of the Norman dukes with their continental neighbors are narrated by A. Fliche, *Le règne de Philippe I^er roi de France* (Paris, 1912); L. Halphen, *Le comté d'Anjou au XI^e siècle* (Paris, 1906); R. Latouche, *Histoire du comté du Maine pendant le X^e et le XI^e siècle* (Paris, 1910); F. Lot, *Fidèles ou vassaux* (Paris, 1904), ch. 6 (on the feudal relations of the Norman dukes and the French kings). There is a good sketch of France in the eleventh century by Luchaire in the *Histoire de France* of Lavisse, II, part 2; a fuller work on this period is expected from Maurice Prou. For the literature of the battle of Hastings, see Gross, *Sources and Literature*, nos. 707a, 2812, 2998–3000; the most important works are those of Round, Spatz, and Delbrück, *Geschichte der Kriegskunst*, III, pp. 147–62 (1907). The Bayeux Tapestry is most conveniently accessible in the small edition of F. R. Fowke (reprinted, London, 1913); see also Gross, no. 2139, and Ph. Lauer, in *Mélanges Charles Bémont* (Paris, 1913), pp. 43–58. Freeman discusses the results of the Conquest in his fifth volume; see also Gaston Paris, *L'esprit normand en Angleterre*, in *La poésie du moyen âge*, second series (Paris, 1895), pp. 45–74.

# IV

THE lecture upon Normandy and England sought to place in their Norman perspective the events leading to the Norman Conquest and to show how that decisive triumph of Norman strength and daring was made possible by the development of an exceptional ducal authority in Normandy and Maine and by the personal greatness of William the Conqueror. We now come to follow still further this process of expansion, to the Scotch border, to Ireland, to the Pyrenees, until the empire of the Plantagenet kings became the chief political fact in western Europe. The Norman empire is the outstanding feature of the twelfth century, as the conquest of England was of the eleventh.

This great imperial state is commonly known, not as the Norman, but as the Angevin, empire, because its rulers, Henry II, Richard, and John, were descended in the male line from the counts of Anjou. The phrase is, however, a misnomer, since it leads one to suppose that the Angevin counts were its creators, which is in no sense the case. The centre of the empire was Normandy, its founders were the Norman dukes. The marriage of the Princess Matilda to Count Geoffrey Plantagenet added

Anjou to Normandy rather than Normandy to Anjou, and it was as duke of Normandy that their son Henry II began his political career. The extension of his domains southward by marriage only gave Normandy the central position in his realm, and it was the loss of Normandy under John which led to the empire's collapse.

Against the application of the term 'empire' to the dominion of Henry II more cogent reasons may be urged. It rests, so far as I know, upon no contemporary authority, and even if the phrase could be found by some chance in a writer of the twelfth century, it would carry with it no weight. Western Europe in the Middle Ages knew but one empire, the Holy Roman Empire of the German Nation — from one point of view neither holy nor Roman nor an empire, as Voltaire long afterward remarked, yet, as revived by Charlemagne and Otto the Great, representing to the mind of the Middle Ages the idea of universal monarchy which they had inherited from ancient Rome. To the men of the twelfth century the emperor was Frederick Barbarossa; he could not be Henry II. Nor will the government of the Norman-Angevin ruler square with the modern definition of an empire as "a state formed by the rule of one state over other states."[1]  His various dominions, if we except Ireland, were not dependencies of England, or Anjou, or Normandy. King in England, duke in Normandy,

[1] W. S. Ferguson, *Greek Imperialism*, p. 1.

count in Anjou and Maine, duke again in Aquitaine, Henry ruled each of his dominions as its feudal lord — very much as if the German Emperor to-day combined in himself the titles of king of Prussia and of Bavaria, grand duke of Baden, duke of Brunswick, prince of Waldeck, and so on throughout the members of the German confederation. Such a government is not an empire in the sense of the ancient Roman or the modern British empires, for it has no dependencies. It is an empire only in the broader and looser sense of the word, a great composite state, larger than a mere kingdom and imperial in extent if not in organization.

That Henry's realm was in extent imperial can easily be seen from the map. It extended from Scotland to the frontier of Spain, as the empire of his contemporary Frederick I extended from the Baltic and the North Sea to central Italy. And if the kingdoms of Germany, Italy, and Burgundy which made up Frederick's empire covered in the aggregate more territory, the actual authority of the ruler, whether in army, justice, or finance, was decidedly less than in the Anglo-Norman state. Henry had a stronger army, a larger revenue, a more centralized government. Moreover, the Norman empire was less artificial than it seems to us at first sight, accustomed as we are to the associations of the modern map. There was, especially with mediæval methods of communication, nothing anomalous in a state which straddled the English Channel: Normandy was nearer England than was Ireland; it was quite as easy to go from London to Rouen as from London to York. The geographical bonds were also strong between Henry's continental dominions, for the roads of the twelfth century did not radiate from Paris, but followed mainly the old Roman lines, and from Rouen there was direct and easy connection with LeMans, Tours, Poitiers, and Bordeaux. In the matter of race, too, we must beware of being misled by our modern ideas. The English nation was at most only the vaguest sort of a conception, the French nation did not exist till the fifteenth century, and personal loyalty to the lord of many different lands was a natural expression of the conditions of the age. It is contrary to our prejudices that a single state should be formed out of the hard-headed Norman, the Celtic fisherman of the Breton coast, — the 'Pêcheur d'Islande' of a later day, — the Angevin, Tourangeau, Poitevin, the troubadour of Aquitaine, and the Gascon of the far south, with his alien blood and non-Aryan language, already a well-marked type whose swaggering gasconades foreshadow the d'Artagnan of the *Three Musketeers* and the 'cadets de Gascogne' of *Cyrano de Bergerac*. But it was little harder to rule these diverse lands from London or Rouen than from Paris; it was for the time being as easy to make them part of a Norman empire as of a French kingdom. Over the various languages and dialects ran the Latin of law and government and the French of the court and of affairs; while in political matters these countries were, as we shall see, quite capable of united action.

Let us call to mind how the empire of Henry II was formed. At the death of the Conqueror in 1087 the lands which he had brought together and ruled with such good peace were divided between his two eldest sons, Robert receiving Normandy and William the Red, England. Save for William's regency over Normandy during his brother's absence on the Crusade, the two countries remained separate during his reign, and were united once more only in 1106 when William's successor, his younger brother Henry I, after defeating and deposing Robert at Tinchebrai, ruled as duke of Normandy and king of England. This was the inheritance which, after the death of Prince William in the White Ship, Henry sought to hand down to his daughter Matilda, but which passed for the most part to his nephew Stephen of Blois. Stephen, however, never gained a firm hold in England and soon lost Normandy to Matilda's husband, Count Geoffrey of Anjou, by whom it was conquered and ruled in the name of his son Henry, later Henry II. Crowned duke of Normandy in 1150, Henry succeeded his father as count of Anjou in the following year, and at Stephen's death in 1154 became king of England. Meanwhile, in 1152, he had contracted a marriage of the greatest political importance with Eleanor, duchess of Aquitaine, whose union with the French king Louis VII had just been annulled by the

Pope; an alliance which made him master of Poitou, Aquitaine, and Gascony and therewith of two-thirds of France. Apart from certain adjustments in central France, the only addition to these territories made during Henry's reign was the conquest of eastern Ireland in the years following 1169. Into these Irish campaigns and their consequences for the whole later history of the island we cannot attempt to go. Let me only point out that the leading spirits were Norman, except so far as they were Irish exiles, and that the names which now make their appearance in Irish annals are Norman names — the Lacys and the Clares, the Fitzgeralds and the de Courcys, as Irish before long as the Irish themselves.

Substantially, then, the empire of Henry II remained in extent as he found it at his accession to the English throne at the age of twenty-one; it was not created by him but inherited or annexed by marriage. Accordingly it is not as a conqueror but as a ruler that he can lay claim to greatness. But although Henry attempted little in the way of acquiring new territory, he did much to consolidate his possessions and to extend his European power and influence. His daughters were married to the greatest princes of their time, Henry the Lion, duke of Saxony and Bavaria, King Alphonso VIII of Castile, King William II of Sicily. He made an alliance with the ruler of Provence and planned a marriage with the house of Savoy that would have given him control of the passes into Italy. He took his part in the struggle of Pope and anti-Pope, of Pope and Emperor; he corresponded with the emperor of Constantinople, refused the crown of the kingdom of Jerusalem, and died on the eve of his departure on a crusade. No one could lay claim to greater influence upon the international affairs of his time.

Occupying this international position, Henry must not be viewed, as he generally is, merely as an English king. He was born and educated on the Continent, began to reign on the Continent, and spent a large part of his life in his continental dominions. He ruled more territory outside of England than in, and his continental lands had at least as large a place as England in his policy. It is perhaps too much to say, in modern phrase, that he 'thought imperially,' but he certainly did not think nationally; and when his latest biographer speaks of Henry's continental campaigns as "foreign affairs,"[1] he is thinking insularly, for Normandy, Anjou, Gascony even, were no more foreign than England itself. Henry is not a national figure, either English or French; he is international, if not cosmopolitan. Only from the point of view of later times can we associate him peculiarly with English history, when after the collapse of the Norman empire under his sons, the permanent influence of his work continued to be felt most fully in England.

[1] Salzmann, *Henry II*, where the continental aspects of Henry's reign are dismissed in a brief chapter on "foreign affairs." The heading would be more appropriate to the account of Henry's campaigns in Ireland.

Both as a man and as a ruler, the figure of Henry II has come down to us distorted by the loves and hates of an age of the most violent and bitter controversy. Brilliant though scarcely heroic to his friends, to his enemies he was a veritable demon of tyranny and crime, whose lurid end pointed many a moral respecting the sins of princes and the vengeance of the Most High. Eminently a strong man, he was not regarded as in any sense superhuman, but rather as an intensely human figure, tempted in all points like as other men and yielding where they yielded. Heavy, bull-necked, sensual, with a square jaw, freckled face, reddish hair, and fiery eyes that blazed in sudden paroxysms of anger, he must, in Bishop Stubbs's phrase, "have looked generally like a rough, passionate, uneasy man."[1] The dominant impression is one of exhaustless energy accompanied by a physical restlessness which kept him whispering and scribbling during mass, hunting and hawking from morning to night, and riding constantly from place to place throughout his vast dominions with a rapidity that always took his enemies by surprise. On one occasion he covered one hundred and seventy miles in two days. Well-educated for a prince of his time and able to hold his own in ready converse with the clerks of his court, his tastes were neither speculative nor romantic, but were early turned toward practical life. He was primarily "an able, plausible, astute, cautious, unprincipled

---

[1] *Benedict of Peterborough*, II, p. xxxiii.

man of business,"[1] fond of work and delighting in detail, with a distinct gift for organization and a mastery of diplomacy, wise in the selection of his subordinates, skilful in evasion, but quick and sure in action. Strong, clear-headed, and tenacious, Henry represents the type of the man of large affairs, and in another age might have amassed a large private fortune as a successful business man. In the twelfth century the chief opportunity for talent of this sort was in public life, where the king's household was also the government of the state, the strengthening of royal authority was the surest means of attaining national unity and security, and the interest of the king coincided with the interest of the state. To the present day, with its cry for business men in public office, this seems natural enough; but we must remember that feudalism meant exactly the opposite of business efficiency, and that the problem of creating an effective government in the midst of a feudal society turned largely on the maintenance of a businesslike administration of justice, finance, and the army. By his success in these fields Henry went a long way toward creating a modern state, and did, as a matter of fact, establish the most highly organized and effective government of its time in western Europe.

Our conceptions of the nature of Henry II's public work have been in certain respects modified as the result of modern research. It has become clear, in the first

---

[1] *Benedict of Peterborough*, II, p. xxxi.

place, that he was an administrator rather than a legis-
lator, and that such of his legislation as has reached us
belongs in the category of instructions to his officers
rather than in that of general enactments. These measures lack the permanence of statutes; they are supplemented, modified, withdrawn, in accordance with the
will of a sovereign whose restless temper showed itself
in a constant series of legal and administrative experiments. Many of his changes seem to have been effected
through oral command rather than written instructions.
In the second place, Henry's originality has been somewhat diminished by a more careful study of the work of
his predecessors, notably of Henry I, in whose reign it
is now possible to trace at work some of the elements
that were once supposed to have been innovations of
his grandson. As a whole, however, the work of
Henry II stands the test of analysis and gives him an
eminent place in the number of mediæval statesmen.

Precocious in many ways as was the political organization of Henry's dominions, it was conditioned by the
circumstances of its time, and we must be careful to
conceive it in terms of the twelfth century and not of the
fifteenth or the twentieth. The Norman sovereign had
at his disposal none of the legal or bureaucratic traditions which were still maintained at Constantinople and
were not without their influence upon the Norman
kingdom of Sicily. Nor was the time ripe for the creation

out of hand of a strong central government for his various territories, such as became possible in the Burgundian state of the fifteenth century and in the Austrian state which was modelled upon it. Henry was in the midst of a feudal society and had to make the best of it. He had to reckon with the particularistic traditions of his several dominions as well as with the feudal opposition to strong government, and western Europe was still a long way from the economic conditions which lie at the basis of modern bureaucracies.

When we speak of the Anglo-Norman or the Angevin empire, we must accordingly dismiss from our minds at the outset any notion of a government with a capital, a central treasury and judicature, and a common assembly. A fixed central treasury existed only in the most advanced of the individual states, and it was many years before the courts established themselves permanently at Westminster and Rouen. Government was still something personal, centring in the person of the sovereign, and the ministers of the state were still his household servants. The king had no fixed residence, and as he moved from place to place, his household and its officers moved with him. Indeed kings were just beginning to learn that it was safer to leave their treasure in some strong castle than to carry it about in their wanderings; it was not till 1194 that the capture of his baggage train by Richard the Lion-Hearted taught the French king Philip Augustus to leave his money and his title-deeds at Paris when he went on a military expedition. We must not be surprised to find that the principal common element in Henry's empire was Henry himself, supplemented by his most immediate household officers, and that many of these officers, such as the seneschals and the justiciars, were limited in their functions to England or Normandy or Anjou, and usually remained in their particular country to look after affairs in the king's absence. There was, however, one notable exception, the chancellor, or royal secretary. Regularly an ecclesiastic, so that there was no chance of his turning the office into an hereditary fief, the nature of the chancellor's duties attached him continuously to the person of the sovereign and made him the natural companion of the royal journeys. He was far, however, from being a mere private secretary or amanuensis, but stood at the head of a regular secretarial bureau, which had its clerks and chaplains and its well-organized system of looking after the king's business. The study of the history of institutions goes to show that, on the whole, there is no better test of the strength or weakness of a mediæval government than its chancery. If it had no chancery, as was the case under the early Norman dukes, or if its methods, as seen in its formal acts, were irregular and unbusinesslike, as under Robert Curthose, there was sure to be a lack of organization and continuity in its general conduct of affairs. If, on the other hand, the chancery was well organized, its rules and practices regularly observed, its documents clear and sharp and to the point, this meant normally that an efficient government stood behind it.

Now, judged by the most exacting standards, the chancery of Henry II had reached a high degree of perfection. It has quite recently been the subject of an elaborate study by the most eminent mediævalist of our time, the late Léopold Delisle, who cannot restrain his admiration for its regularity, its accuracy and finish, and the extraordinary range and rapidity of its work. The documents issued in the name of Henry II during his long reign of thirty-five years, says Delisle,[1] "both for his English and his continental possessions, are all drawn up on the same plan in identical formulæ and expressed with irreproachable precision in a simple, clear, and correct style, which is also remarkably uniform save for a small number of pieces which show the hand of others than the royal officers." If the judgment of this master required support, I should be glad to confirm it from the personal examination of some hundreds of Henry's charters and writs. Such uniformity, it should be observed, is evidence not only of the extent and technical attainments of the chancery but of substantially similar administrative conditions throughout the various dominions to which these documents are addressed: officers, functions, legal and administrative procedure are everywhere very much alike. Moreover, a study of

[1] *Recueil des actes de Henri II*, Introduction, p. 1; cf. p. 151.

these charters reveals another fact of fundamental importance. Even more significant than uniformity of procedure in a chancery is the type of document issued, for since the strength of government lies not in legislation but in administration, a sure index of a state's efficiency will be found in the extent and character of its administrative correspondence. This test places the Norman empire far in advance of any of its contemporaries. Every payment from the treasury, every allowance of an account, every summons to the army, every executive command or prohibition, was made by formal royal writ — *per breve regis*, as we read page after page in the account rolls. Of the many thousands of such writs issued in Henry's reign, exceedingly few have come down to us, but no one can read these, terse, direct, trained down to bone and muscle, without realizing the keen minds and the clear-cut administrative methods which they represent. Take an example: [1]

H. Dei gratia rex Anglorum et dux Normannorum et Aquitanorum et comes Andegavorum R. thesaurario et Willelmo Malduit et Warino filio Giroldi camerariis suis salutem.

Liberate de thesauro meo xxv marcas fratribus Cartusie de illis L marcis quas do eis annuatim per cartam meam.

Teste Willelmo de Sancte Marie Ecclesia. Apud Westmoster.

The purpose of these writs might, of course, vary — seize A of this land; do right to B for that tenement;

---

[1] Delisle, p. 166, from Madox, *Exchequer*, I, p. 390.

secure C in his possession; bring your knights to such a place at such a time; summon twelve men to decide D's right; — but each has its appropriate form, which is always crisp and exact. All speak the language of a strong, businesslike administration which expected as a matter of course prompt and implicit obedience throughout its broad dominions.

If such a system be given enough time, it will inevitably exert a strong and persistent influence in favor of centralization and uniformity, and it would be interesting to know just what was accomplished in these directions during the half century of the Norman empire's existence. The parting advice which Henry had received from his father Geoffrey was to avoid the transfer of customs and institutions from one part of his realm to another, and the wisdom of the warning was obvious under feudal conditions, if not in all imperial governments. But there is a difference between the field of local custom and the institutions of administration, and while even in matters of feudal law there is some evidence of a generalization of certain reforms in the rules of succession, in the conduct of government it was impossible to keep the different parts of the empire in water-tight compartments so long as there was a common administration and frequent interchange of officials between different regions. We must remember that Henry was a constant experimenter, and that if a thing worked well in one place it was likely to be tried in another. Thus the Assize of Arms and the ordinance for the crusading tithe were first promulgated for his continental dominions, while the great English inquest of knights' fees in 1166 preceded by six years the parallel Norman measure. The great struggle with Becket over the church courts seems to have had a Norman prologue. The chronological order in any given case might well be a matter of chance; but in administrative matters the influence is likely to have travelled from the older and better organized to the newer and more loosely knit dominions, from England, Normandy, and Anjou on the one hand to Poitou, Aquitaine, and Gascony on the other.

Of Henry's hereditary territories, Anjou seems the least important from the point of view of constitutional influence. Much smaller in area than either Normandy or England, it was a compact and comparatively centralized state long before Henry's accession, but the opportunity for immediate action on the count's part simplified its government to a point where its experience was of no great value under Anglo-Norman conditions. Certainly no Angevin influence is traceable in the field of finance, and none seems probable in the administration of justice. In the case of Normandy and England the resemblance of institutions is closest, and a host of interesting problems present themselves which carry us back to the effects of the Norman Conquest and even further.

It is, of course, one of the fundamental problems of English history how far the government of England was Normanized in the century following the Conquest. To a French scholar like Boutmy everything begins anew in 1066, when "the line which the whole history of political institutions has subsequently followed was traced and defined." [1] To Freeman, on the other hand, the changes then introduced were temporary and not fundamental. He is never tired of repeating that the old English are the real English; progress comes by going back to the principles of the Anglo-Saxon period and casting aside innovations which have crept in in modern and evil times; "we have advanced by falling back on a more ancient state of things, we have reformed by calling to life again the institutions of earlier and ruder times, by setting ourselves free from the slavish subtleties of Norman lawyers, by casting aside as an accursed thing the innovations of Tudor tyranny and Stewart usurpation." [2] The trend of present scholarly opinion lies between these extremes. It refuses to throw away the Anglo-Saxon period, whose institutions we are just beginning to read aright; but it rejects its idealization at Freeman's hands, who, it has been said, saw all things "through a mist of moots and witans" and not as they really were, and it finds more truth in Carlyle's remark that the pot-bellied equanimity of the Anglo-Saxon

[1] *The English Constitution*, p. 3.
[2] *Origin of the English Constitution* (London, 1872), p. 20 *f*.

needed the drilling and discipline of a century of Norman tyranny.[1]

Whether he was needed much or little, the Norman drill-master came and did his work, and when he had finished the two countries were in many respects alike. He left his mark on the English language and on English literature, which were submerged for three centuries under the French of the court, the castle, and the town, and in the process were permanently modified into a mixed speech. He left his mark on architecture in the great cathedrals of the Norman bishops and the massive castles with their Norman keeps. He made England a feudal society, however far it may have gone in that direction before, and its law, from that day to this, a feudal law. And he remade the central government under the strong hand of a masterful dynasty which compelled its subjects to will what the king willed. Whatever permanence we may assign to Anglo-Saxon local institutions, — and we cannot help granting them this in considerable measure, — it is not now held that there was any notable Anglo-Saxon influence upon the central administration. At best England before the Conquest was a loose aggregation of tribal commonwealths divided by local feeling and by the jealousies of the great earls, and its kingship did not grow stronger with process of time. The national assembly of wise men, whose persistence Freeman labored in vain to prove, became the feudal

[1] Stubbs, *Benedict of Peterborough*, II, p. xxxv.

council of the Norman barons, and this council, the
*curia regis*, and the royal household which was its permanent nucleus, became the starting-point of a new
constitutional development which produced the House
of Lords, the courts of law, and the great departments
of the central administration.

Yet in a vigorous state central and local are never
wholly separable, and it is where they touch that recent study has been able to show some continuity of
development between the two periods, namely in the
fiscal system which culminated in the exchequer of
the English kings. Of all the institutions of the Anglo-
Norman state, none is more important and none more
characteristic than the exchequer, illustrating as it does
at the same time the comparative wealth of the sovereigns and the efficient conduct of their government. Nowhere in western Europe did a king receive so large a
revenue as here; nowhere was it collected and administered in so regular and businesslike a fashion; nowhere
do the accounts afford so complete a view of "the whole
framework of society." The main features of this system are simple and striking.

In every administrative district of Normandy and
England the king had an agent — in England the sheriff,
in Normandy the *vicomte* or *bailli*—to collect his revenues, which consisted chiefly of the income from lands
and forests, the fees and fines in the royal courts, the

proceeds of the various feudal incidents, and the various payments which there were from time to time levied under the name of Danegeld, scutage, aid, or gift. Twice a year, at Easter and Michaelmas, these agents were required to come to the treasury and render their accounts to the king's officers. At Easter the sheriff was expected to pay in half of his receipts, receiving therefor down to 1826 a receipt in the form of a notched stick or tally, split down the middle so that there was exact agreement between the portion retained at the exchequer and the portion carried off by the sheriff to be produced when the acounts of the year were settled at Michaelmas. The great session of the exchequer at Michaelmas was a very important occasion and is described for us in detail in a most interesting contemporary treatise, the *Dialogue on the Exchequer*, written by Richard the King's Treasurer, in 1178–79. There the sheriff met the great officials of the king's household who were also the great officers of the Anglo-Norman state — the justiciar, chancellor, constable, treasurer, chamberlains, and marshal, reënforced by clerks, tally-cutters, calculators, and other assistants. The place and the institution took their names from a chequered table or chessboard—the Latin name *scaccarium* means a chess-board — in size and shape not unlike a billiard table, covered with cloth which was ruled off into columns for pence, shillings, pounds, hundreds and thousands of pounds. On one side were set forth in this graphic manner the sums

which the sheriff was required to pay, on the other he
and his clerk tried to offset these with tallies, receipts,
warrants, and counters representing actual cash. Played
with skill and care on each side, for the stakes were high,
this great match was likened to a game of chess between
the sheriff and the king's officers. Its results were recorded
each year, district by district and item by item, on a
great roll, called the pipe roll from the pipes, or skins of
parchment sewed end to end, of which it was made up.
For England we have an unbroken series of these rolls
from the second year of Henry II, as well as an odd roll
of Henry I, constituting a record of finance and government quite unique in contemporary Europe. The series
was doubtless as complete for Normandy, but there survive from Henry's reign only the roll of 1180 and fragments of that of 1184. For the other Plantagenet lands
nothing remains.

This remarkable fiscal system comprised accordingly
a regular method of collecting revenue, a central treasury and board of account, and a distinctive and careful mode of auditing the accounts. There was nothing
like it north of Sicily, and contemporaries admired it
both for its administrative efficiency and for the wealth
and resources which it implied. Although something
of the sort seems to have existed in all the territories of
the Plantagenet empire and the different bodies seem
to have maintained a certain amount of coöperation,
all our records come from England and Normandy,

and there can be no question that it is distinctively an Anglo-Norman institution. Whether, however, it is English or Norman in origin and how it came into existence, are still in many respects obscure questions. The exchequer is not an innovation of Henry II, for the surviving roll of Henry I and certain incidental evidence show that it existed on both sides of the Channel in the reign of his grandfather. In the time of the author of the *Dialogue* there was a tradition that it had been imported from Normandy by William the Conqueror, but this must be discounted by the fact that certain elements of the system can be traced in Anglo-Saxon England. The truth is that the exchequer is a complicated institution, some parts of which may be quite ancient and the results of parallel development on both sides of the Channel; at least the problem of priority has reached no certain solution. Its most characteristic feature, however, its peculiar method of reckoning, does not seem either of Norman or English origin, but derived from the abacus of the ancient Romans, as used and taught in the continental schools of the eleventh and twelfth centuries.

One who tries to perform with Roman numerals a simple problem in addition or subtraction — or better yet, in multiplication or division — will have no difficulty in understanding why people unacquainted with the Arabic system of notation have had recourse to a counting-machine or abacus. The difficulty, of course, lies not so much in the clumsy form of the individual Roman numbers as in the absence of the zero and the reckoning by position which it makes possible. This defect the abacus supplied. By means of a sanded board or a cloth-covered table or a string of counters it provided a row of columns each of which represented a decimal group — units, tens, hundreds, etc. — by which numerical operations could be rapidly and accurately performed. Employed by the ancient Romans, as by the modern Chinese, the arithmetic of the abacus became a regular subject of instruction in the schools of the Middle Ages, whence its reckoning was introduced into the operations of the Anglo-Norman treasury. The most recent student of the subject, Reginald Lane Poole, connects the change with the Englishmen who studied at the cathedral school of Laon early in the twelfth century. To me it seems somewhat earlier, brought by abacists who came to England in the eleventh century from the schools of Lorraine.[1] In either case its introduction was much more than a change of bookkeeping. Convenient as such reckoning was in general, it was the only possible method for men who could neither read nor write, like the Anglo-Norman sheriffs and many of the royal officers, and its use made it possible to carry on the fiscal business of the state on a large scale, in an open and public fashion,

[1] Poole, *The Exchequer in the Twelfth Century*, pp. 42–57; Haskins, "The Abacus and the King's Curia," in *English Historical Review*, xxvII, pp. 101–06.

with full justice to all parties, and with accuracy, certainty, and dispatch. It was a businesslike system for busy and businesslike men.

In the history of judicial administration the personal initiative of Henry II is more evident than in finance. The king had an especial fondness for legal questions and often participated in their decision, yet his influence was exerted particularly to develop a system of courts and judges which could work in his absence and without his intervention. Although the institution is found previously both in England and Normandy, it is in Henry's reign that the system of itinerant justices is fully organized with regular circuits and a rapidly extending jurisdiction which broke down local privileges and exemptions and by its decisions created the common law. Hitherto chiefly a feudal assembly concerned with the causes of the king and his barons, after Henry's time the king's court is a permanent body of professional judges and a tribunal for the whole realm. It is no accident that his reign produced in the treatise of Glanvill on *The Laws and Customs of England* the first of the great series of textbooks which are the landmarks of English legal development. Henry's reign is also an important period in the growth of Norman law, the earliest formulation of which reaches us ten years after his death in the *Très Ancien Coutumier de Normandie*, and the reduction of local custom to writing is a process which went on in his other continental possessions; yet, as in finance, England and Normandy plainly took the lead in legal literature and in legal development. Indeed, the distinction between justice and finance is less sharp than we might at first suppose, for the growth of jurisdiction meant increased profit from fees and fines, and heavy payments were necessary to secure the intervention of the royal judges. In this sense Henry has often been called, and rightly, a seller of justice, but his latest biographer has pointed out that "if the commodity was expensive it was at least the best of its kind, and there is a profound gulf between the selling of justice and of injustice. A bribe might be required to set the machine of the law in motion, but it would be unavailing to divert its course when once started." [1] The wheels of government are turned by self-interest as well as by unselfish statesmanship.

Of the many judicial reforms of Henry's reign none is more significant than the measures which he took for extending the use of the jury as a method of trial in the royal courts, and none illustrates better the relation of Norman to English institutions. Characteristic as the jury is in the history of English government and of English law, as at once the palladium of personal liberty and the basis of representative institutions in Parliament, it is a striking fact that originally it was "not popular but royal," not English but Norman, or rather

[1] Salzmann, *Henry II*, p. 176.

Frankish through the intermediary of Normandy.[1]
Although it has a history which can be traced for more
than a thousand years, the jury does not definitely make
its appearance in England until after the Norman Conquest, and the decisive steps in its further development
were taken during the union of England and Normandy
and probably as a result of Norman experience. It is
now the general opinion of scholars that the modern
jury is an outgrowth of the sworn inquests of neighbors
held by command of the Norman and Angevin kings,
and that the procedure in these inquests is in all essen-
tial respects the same as that employed by the Frankish
rulers three centuries before. It is also generally agreed
that while such inquests appear in England immedi-
ately after the Norman Conquest, — the returns of the
Domesday survey are a striking example, — their employment in lawsuits remains exceptional until the
time of Henry II, when they become in certain cases a
matter of right and a part of the settled law of the land.
What had been heretofore a special privilege of the
king and of those to whom he granted it, became under
Henry a right of his subjects and a part of the regular
system of justice. Accomplished doubtless gradually,
first for one class of cases and then for another, this extension of the king's prerogative procedure to his subjects seems to have been formulated in a definite royal
act or series of acts, probably by royal ordinances or

[1] Pollock and Maitland, *History of English Law*, I, p. 142.

assizes, whence the procedure is often called the assize. In England the earliest of these assizes known to us appears in 1164 in the Constitutions of Clarendon, followed shortly by applications of this mode of trial to other kinds of cases. In Normandy repeated references to similar assizes occur some years earlier, between 1156 and 1159, so that as far as present evidence goes, the priority of Normandy in this respect is clear. Moreover, Normandy offers two pieces of evidence that are still earlier. In the oldest cartulary of Bayeux cathedral, called the *Black Book* and still preserved high up in one of its ancient towers, are two writs of the duke ordering his justices to have determined by sworn inquest, in accordance with the duke's assize, the facts in dispute between the bishop of Bayeux and certain of his tenants. The ducal initial was left blank when these writs were copied into the cartulary, in order that it might later be inserted in colors by an illuminator who never came; and those who first studied these documents drew the hasty conclusion that they were issued by Henry as duke of Normandy before he became king. It was not, however, usual for the mediæval scribe to leave the rubricator entirely without guidance when he came to insert his initials, but to mark the proper letter lightly in the place itself or on the margin, and an attentive examination of the well-thumbed margins of the Bayeux *Black Book* shows that this was no exception to the rule, and that in both the cases in question the initial G had been carefully indicated. G can, of course, stand only for Henry's father Geoffrey, so that some general use of the assize as a method of trial in the ducal courts can be proved for his reign. As no such documents have reached us for his predecessors, it would be tempting to assume the influence of Angevin precedents; but this runs counter to what we know of the judicial institutions of Anjou in this period, as well as of the policy of Geoffrey in Normandy, which was to follow in all respects the system of Henry I. Although the first general use of the sworn inquest as a mode of trial thus antedates Henry II, it is still a Norman institution.

It would carry us too far to discuss the many problems connected with the use of the jury in Henry's reign or to follow the many changes still needed to convert the sworn inquest into the modern jury. It is sufficient for our present purpose to mark its Norman character, first as being carried to England by the Normans in its older form, and then as being developed into its newer form on Norman soil. It should, however, be remembered that its later history belongs to England rather than to Normandy. With the rise of new forms of procedure in the thirteenth century, the jury on the Continent declines and finally disappears; "but for the conquest of England," says Maitland, "it would have perished and long ago have become a matter for the antiquary." [1] In England, however, it was early brought into relations with the local courts of the hundred and the county, where it struck root and developed into a popular method of trial which was later to become a defence against the king's officers who had first introduced it. A bulwark of individual liberty, the jury also holds an important place in the establishment of representative government, for it was through representative juries that the voice of the countryside first asserted itself in the local courts, for the assessment of taxes as well as for the decision of cases, and it was in the negotiations of royal officers with the local juries that we can trace the beginnings of the House of Commons. It is no accident that the first employment of local juries for the assessment of military and fiscal obligations belongs to the later years of Henry II.

It may seem a far cry from the Frankish inquests of the ninth century to the juries and the representative assemblies of the twentieth, but the development is continuous, and it leads through Normandy. In this sense the English-speaking countries are all heirs of the early Normans and of the Norman kings who, all unconsciously, provided for the extension and the perpetuation of the Norman methods of trial. At such points Norman history merges in that of England, the British Empire, and the United States.

[1] Pollock and Maitland, I, p. 141.

## BIBLIOGRAPHICAL NOTE

The chief events in the history of the Norman empire are treated in the general works of Miss K. L. Norgate, *England under the Angevin Kings* (London, 1887); Sir J. H. Ramsay, *The Angevin Empire* (London, 1903); G. B. Adams, *History of England from the Norman Conquest to the Death of John* (London, 1905); H. W. C. Davis, *England under the Normans and Angevins* (London, 1905). There is a brief biography of *Henry the Second* by Mrs. J. R. Green (London, 1888; reprinted, 1903); and a more recent one by L. F. Salzmann (Boston, etc., 1914). A notable characterization of Henry and his work is given by William Stubbs, in the introduction to his edition of *Benedict of Peterborough*, II (London, 1867), reprinted in his *Historical Introductions* (London, 1902), pp. 89–172. For the continental aspects of the reign see F. M. Powicke, *The Loss of Normandy* (Manchester, 1913); and his articles in the *English Historical Review*, XXI, XXII (1906–07). Cf. A. Cartellieri, *Die Machtstellung Heinrichs II. von England*, in *Neue Heidelberger Jahrbücher*, VIII, pp. 269–83 (1898); F. Hardegen, *Imperialpolitik König Heinrichs II. von England* (Heidelberg, 1905). The fullest account of Irish affairs is G. H. Orpen, *Ireland under the Normans* (Oxford, 1911).

The best general accounts of constitutional and legal matters are those of Stubbs, *Constitutional History of England*, I (last edition, Oxford, 1903), corrected by various special studies of J. H. Round, to be found chiefly in his *Feudal England* (London, 1895; reprinted, 1909) and *Commune of London* (Westminster, 1899); and by Pollock and Maitland, *History of English Law* (second edition, London, 1898). The results of recent investigation are incorporated in the studies and notes appended to the French translation of Stubbs by Petit-Dutaillis (Paris, 1907); this supplementary material is translated into English by W. E. Rhodes (Manchester, 1911). There are admirable studies of the chancery in L. Delisle, *Recueil des actes de Henri II concernant les provinces françaises et les affaires de France*, introduction (Paris, 1909); and of the exchequer in R. L. Poole, *The Exchequer in the Twelfth Century* (Oxford, 1912). See also Hubert Hall, *Court Life under the Plantagenets* (London, 1890; reprinted, 1902). For the more distinctively Norman side of the government see Haskins, "The Government of Normandy under Henry II," in *American Historical Review*, xx, pp. 24–42, 277–91 (1914–15); and earlier papers on "The Early Norman Jury," *ibid.*, VIII, pp. 613–40 (1903); "The Administration of Normandy under Henry I," in *English Historical Review*, XXIV, pp. 209–31 (1909); "Normandy under Geoffrey Plantagenet," *ibid.*, XXVII, pp. 417–44 (1912); Delisle, *Des revenus publics en Normandie au XII^e siècle*, in *Bibliothèque de l'École des Chartes*, X–XIII (1848–52); Valin, *Le duc de Normandie et sa cour*, supplemented by R. de Fréville, "Étude sur l'organisation judiciaire en Normandie aux XII^e et XIII^e siècles," in *Nouvelle Revue historique de droit*, 1912, pp. 681–736. The best general account of Norman law is still that of H. Brunner, *Die Entstehung der Schwurgerichte* (Berlin, 1872).

# V

## NORMANDY AND FRANCE

IN July, 1189, Henry II lay dying in his castle at Chinon. Abandoned and attacked by his sons, driven from LeMans and Tours by Philip of France and forced to a humiliating peace, sick in body and broken in spirit, the aged king made his way to the old stronghold of the Angevin counts in the valley of the Vienne. Cursing the faithless Richard as he gave him the enforced kiss of peace at Colombières, he had fixed his hopes on his youngest son John till the schedule was brought him of those who had thrown off their allegiance. "Sire," said the clerk who read the document to the fever-tossed king, "may Christ help me, the first here written is Count John, your son." "What," cried the king, starting up from his bed, "John, my very heart, my best beloved, for whose advancement I have brought upon me all this misery? Now let all things go as they will; I care no more for myself nor for anything in this world." Two days later he died, cursing his sons, cursing the day he had been born, repeating constantly, "Shame on a conquered king." Deserted by all save his illegitimate son Geoffrey, who received his father's blessing and his signet ring marked with the leopard of England, Henry was plundered by his attendants of gold and furnishings and apparel, just as William the Conqueror had been despoiled in the hour of his death at Rouen, till some one in pity threw over the royal corpse the short cloak, or 'curt mantle,' by which men called him. Two days later he was laid away quietly in the nunnery of Fontevrault, where a later age was to rob his tomb of all save the noble recumbent figure by which it is still marked. Thus passed away the greatest ruler of his age; thus began the collapse of the Norman empire.

Strikingly dramatic both in its public and private aspects, the end of Henry II offers material fit for a Greek tragedy, and we may, if we choose, imagine an Æschylus or a Sophocles painting the rapidity of his rise, the *hybris* of his splendor, and the crushing *nemesis* of his fall. Even the Promethean touch is not lacking in the withdrawal of Henry's unconquered soul from God, as he looked back in flight at the burning city of Le Mans: "My God, since to crown my confusion and increase my disgrace, thou hast taken from me so vilely the town which on earth I have loved best, where I was born and bred, and where my father lies buried and the body of St. Julian too, I will have my revenge on thee also; I will of a surety withdraw from thee that thing that thou lovest best in me." [1] Henry's life needs no blasphemous closing in order to furnish inexhaustible

[1] Giraldus Cambrensis (Rolls Series), VIII, p. 283.

material for moralizing, and in a period like the Middle Ages, given over as none other to moral lessons, it served to point many a tale of the crimes and fate of evil-doers. That vain and entertaining Welshman, Gerald de Barri, or Giraldus Cambrensis, in whom a recent writer thinks he has discovered the proto-journalist,[1] found in Henry's career the basis for a considerable book devoted to the *Instruction of Princes*. But whereas the ways of the gods are dark and unsearchable to the Greek tragedians, they have no mystery for Gerald. Henry's punishment was due to his violations of religion, first in his marriage with Eleanor, the divorced wife of his feudal lord Louis VII, second in his quarrel with Archbishop Becket and the oppression of the church which followed, and third and worst of all, in his failure to take part in a crusade. The hammer of the church, Henry was born for destruction. The modern world is more cautious in the matter of explaining the inexplicable, and more prone to seek human causes when they can be found, yet the collapse of the Plantagenet empire is not the hardest of the historian's problems. Something he will ascribe to larger forces of development, something he can hardly fail to attribute to the character of Henry's sons and to his policy in dealing with them.

Henry II is not the only case in history of a king who could rule every house but his own, of a father who was

---

[1] Salzmann, *Henry II*, p. 214.

shrewd and stern in his dealings with the world but swayed by unrequited affection and ill-timed weakness in dealing with his children. Knowing other men, he did not know his sons, and his grave errors in dealing with them were errors of public policy, since they concerned the government of his dominions and the succession to the throne. Even those who had no sympathy for Henry had little to say to excuse the character and the unfilial conduct of his sons. "From the Devil we come, and to the Devil we return," Richard was reported to have said; and none cared to contradict him. Of the four lawful sons who grew to maturity, the eldest was Henry, crowned king by his father in 1170, and hence generally known as the Young King. Handsome and agreeable, prodigal in *largesse*, a patron of knightly sports and especially of the tournaments which were then coming into fashion, the Young King enjoyed great popularity in his lifetime and after his early death was mourned as a peer of Hector and Achilles and enshrined as a hero of courtly romance. Yet for all this there was no substantial foundation. He was faithless, ungrateful, utterly selfish, a thorn in his father's side and a constant source of weakness to the empire. Married at the age of five to the daughter of Louis VII, he became the instrument of the French king in his intrigues against Henry II and the rallying point of feudal reaction and personal jealousy. King in name though not in fact, having been crowned merely as a means of securing the succession, Prince Henry craved at least an under-kingdom of his own, and on two occasions, in 1173 and again in 1183, led serious and widespread revolts against his father, the evil results of which were not undone by his death-bed repentance in the midst of the second uprising. In this revolt of 1183 he had with him his younger brother Geoffrey, duke of Brittany, 'the son of perdition,' equally false and treacherous, without even the redeeming virtue of popularity. Fortunately Geoffrey also died before his father.

The death of the Young King left as Henry's eldest heir Richard, known to the modern world as the Lion-Hearted. With much of his father's energy, Richard seems to have inherited more than any of his brothers the tastes and temperament of his mother, Eleanor of Aquitaine. Adventurous and high-spirited, fond of pomp and splendor, a lover of poetry and music, be it the songs of Provençal minstrels or the solemn chants of the church, he belonged on this side of his nature to the dukes of Aquitaine and the country of the troubadours. He loved war and danger, in which he showed great personal courage, and in the conduct of military enterprises gave evidence of marked ability as a strategist; but his gifts as a ruler stopped there. The glamour of his personal exploits and the romance of his crusading adventures might dazzle the imagination of contemporaries more than the prosaic achievements of his father,

and his gifts to religious houses might even predispose
monastic historians in his favor, but for all this splendor
his subjects paid the bills. In spite of his great income,
he was always in need of money for his extravagances;
and for his fiscal exactions there was never the excuse of
large measures of public policy. Indeed, so far as we can
see, Richard had no public policy. "His ambition," says
Stubbs, "was that of a mere warrior: he would fight for
anything whatever, but he would sell everything that
was worth fighting for." [1] Self-willed and self-centred,
he followed wherever his desires led, with no sense of
loyalty to his obligations or of responsibility as a ruler.
Made duke of Aquitaine at seventeen, he sought to ride
down every obstacle and bring immediate order and
unity into a region which had never enjoyed either of
these benefits; and he quickly had by the ears the land
which he should have best understood. He was soon in
revolt against his father and also at war with the Young
King; for his own purposes he later went over to the king
of France, and jested with his boon companions over his
father's discomfiture and downfall. Even as king at the
age of thirty-two, Richard remained an impetuous
youth; he never really grew up. Haughty and overbearing, he alienated friends and allies; inheriting the rule of
the vast Plantagenet empire, he showed no realization of
imperial duty or opportunity. Thus he visited England
but twice in the course of his reign of ten years and

[1] *Constitutional History*, I, p. 551.

valued it solely as a land from which revenue might be wrung by his ministers, nor did his continental dominions derive advantage from his presence. Impetuous and short-sighted, Richard Yea-and-Nay had to meet the greatest statesman of his day in deadly rivalry; and though panegyrists placed him above Alexander, Charlemagne, and King Arthur, he went down ignominiously before Philip Augustus.

Last of all comes the youngest son John, "my heart, my best beloved." Never did father lavish his affection on a more unworthy child. False to his father, false to his brother Richard, John proved false to all, man or woman, who ever trusted him. He had none of the dash and courage of Richard, none of his large and splendid way, and none of his popularity and gift of leadership. Men saw him as he was, no Charlemagne or Arthur, but petty, mean, and cowardly, small even in his blasphemies, swearing by the feet or the teeth of God, when Henry II had habitually sworn by his eyes, and William the Conqueror by his splendor — *par la resplendor De!* Always devious in his ways, John's cunning sometimes got him the reputation for cleverness, and John Richard Green went so far as to call him "the ablest and most ruthless of the Angevins." But his ability, particularly in military matters not inconsiderable, was of the kind which wasted itself in temporary expedients and small successes; it was incapable of continuous policy or sustained efforts; and it everywhere ended in failure. Ger-

ald the Welshman, the friend of his youth, at the end
can only pronounce him the worst of history's tyrants.
John's whole career offers the most convincing evidence
of the futility of talent when divorced from character,
by which is here meant, not so much private virtue, —
for John's private vices were shared with others of his
family and his time, — but merely common honor,
trustworthiness, and steadfastness. Even in his wicked-
ness John was shifty and false, and his loss of his empire
was due, not to any single blunder or series of blunders,
but to the supreme sin of lack of character.

It is thus possible to see how largely the collapse of
the Norman empire was bound up with the family history
of Henry II — the foolish indulgence of the father, the
ambitions and intrigues of the mother, the jealousies,
treachery, and political incapacity of the sons. A personal creation, the Plantagenet state fell in large measure for personal reasons. If it was Henry's misfortune to
have such sons, one may say it was also his misfortune to
have more than one son of any sort, since each became
the nucleus of a separatist movement in some particular
territory. The kings of France, it has often been pointed
out, had for generations the great advantage of having a
son to succeed, but only a single son. The crowning of
the French heir in his father's lifetime assured an undisputed succession; the crowning of the Young King left
him dissatisfied and stirred up the rivalry of his younger
brothers.

But this is not the whole of the story. The very strength and efficiency of Henry's government were sure to produce a reaction in favor of feudal liberties in which his sons serve simply as convenient centres of crystallization. Only time could unify each of these dominions internally, while far more time was required to consolidate them into a permanent kingdom, and these processes were interrupted when they had barely begun. Such a solution of the ultimate problem of consolidation was, we have seen, entirely possible and even natural; but another was possible and also natural, namely the union of these territories under the king of France. Geography, as well as history, favored the second alternative.

The geographical unity of France is one of the most obvious facts on the map of Europe. The Alps and the Pyrenees, the Mediterranean and the Atlantic, are its natural frontiers; only on the northeast are the lines blurred by nature and left to history to determine. Within these limits there are of course many clearly marked subdivisions — the valleys of the Rhone, Garonne, Loire, and Seine, Gascony, Brittany, Normandy, Flanders, and the rest — which formed the great fiefs of the Middle Ages and the great provinces of later times. Sooner or later, however, as population increased, as trade and commerce developed, and as the means of communication were strengthened, these divisions were certain to draw together into a single great state. Where the centre of the new state would lie was not a matter of accident but was largely determined by the great lines of communication, and especially by the commercial axis which runs from the Mediterranean to Flanders and the English Channel. On this line are situated the Roman capital of the Gauls, Lyons, and the modern capital, Paris. This fact, combined with the central and dominant position of the Paris basin in relation to the great valleys of the Seine, the Loire, and the Meuse, established the region about Paris, the Ile-de-France of history, as the natural centre of this future nation. Such a state might grow from without toward its centre, as the modern kingdom of Italy closed in on Rome, but the more natural process was from the centre outward, as England grew about Wessex or Brandenburg about the region near Berlin. In the great contest between Capetian and Plantagenet the Capetian "held the inner lines." Shut off from the sea on the side of the Loire as well as on the side of the Seine, he was in a position to concentrate all his efforts to break through the iron ring, while the Norman rulers had to hold together the whole of their far-spread territories against reaction and rebellion at home as well as against the French at Tours and LeMans and in the Vexin. Meanwhile up and down these valleys the influences of trade, commerce, and travel were at work breaking down the political barriers and drawing the remoter regions toward the geographical centre. The rivers in their courses fought against the Plantagenets.

The personal element in the struggle was weighted against the Anglo-Norman empire even more strongly than the physiographic, for the weak links in the Plantagenet succession ran parallel to the strongest portion of the Capetian line. Against a knight-errant like Richard and a trifler like John, stood a great European statesman in the person of Philip Augustus, king of France during forty-four years, and more than any single man the creator of the French monarchy.

Philip Augustus was not an heroic figure, and to the men of his age he was probably less sympathetic than his adversary Richard. Vigorous and enduring, a generous liver, quick-tempered but slow to cherish hatred, Philip was preëminently the cautious, shrewd, unscrupulous, far-sighted statesman. He could fight when necessary, but he had no great personal courage and excelled in strategy and prevision rather than in tactics or leadership in the field, and he preferred to gain his ends by the arts of diplomacy. The quality upon which all his contemporaries dwell is his wisdom. Throughout his long reign he kept before him as his one aim the increase of the royal power, and by his patient and fortunate efforts he broke down the Plantagenet empire, doubled the royal revenue and more than doubled the royal domain, and made France the leading international power in western Europe.

As we have already seen, Philip had made substantial headway even during the lifetime of Henry II. Crowned in 1179 at the age of fourteen, a year before the death of his paralytic father Louis VII, Philip was naturally treated as a boy by Henry, who seems, however, to have acted throughout with due regard to Philip's position as king and his feudal suzerain. In the complications of those early years we find Henry constantly arranging disputes with the king's vassals and more than once saving him from a tight place. But as time went on this relation became impossible. Philip openly abetted the revolts of the Young King and of Richard, and in the war which broke out at the end Richard fought openly on his side. As soon, however, as Richard succeeded to the throne, Philip began hostilities with him, and he soon used John against Richard as he had used Richard against his father. "Divide and rule," was clearly Philip's policy, and he always had on his side the fact that he was king in France and the Plantagenets on the Continent were his vassals.

The first phase of the contest between Richard and Philip comes as a welcome interlude in the tale of border disputes and family rivalries which make up the greater part of the tangled story of Philip's dealings with the Norman empire. It takes us over the sea to the fair land of Sicily and on to the very gates of the Holy City. In

1187 the capture of Jerusalem had crowned the long efforts of the great Saladin, and where a century before Christian knights had ridden "up to their bridles" in the blood of the slaughtered Moslem, a procession of knights and priests and poorer folk passed out of the gate of David and left the Holy Sepulchre to the infidel. To the Saracens a certain sign that they were the only people "whose doctrine was agreeable to God," the fall of Jerusalem killed the aged Pope, plunged Europe into prayer and fasting, and brought on the Third Crusade, under the leadership of the emperor Frederick Barbarossa, Philip of France, and Richard of England. Richard, then merely count of Poitou, was the first western prince to take the cross in this holy war; his father and Philip soon sealed their crusading vows with a public reconciliation under a great elm on the borders of Normandy and France, and the chroniclers tell us that every man made peace with his neighbor, thinking no more of tournaments and fine raiment, the lust of the flesh and the pride of the eye, but only of the recovery of the Holy City. Such great waves of renunciation and religious enthusiasm are peculiarly characteristic of the Middle Ages, but their force was soon spent. Then, as in other times, there were few who could live as on a mountain-top. In spite of all that the church could do, Henry and Philip soon came to open war, and the cause of Jerusalem was swallowed up in a struggle for the Loire and for Aquitanian fortresses. Richard, as we have seen,

was a central point in these conflicts, and his accession
to the throne simply continued the struggle in another
form.

Nevertheless a peace was patched up, and the unwilling Philip was unable to hold aloof from the crusade
which fired the military ardor of his chief vassal and
rival. Large sums of money were raised by every means,
and the two kings made an agreement to divide equally
all the spoil of their expedition. They also arranged to
go by sea to the East after they had assembled their
ships and followers at Messina, thus avoiding the usual
complications with the Eastern Empire and the fatal
march through the barren and hostile interior of Asia
Minor which now claimed another victim in the gallant
German emperor. At the best, however, a crusade was
not an organized campaign under efficient direction, but
merely a number of independent expeditions which
found it convenient to go at the same time and by the
same route. There was no supreme command, and there
was constant jealousy and friction between feudal lords
who were ever impatient of restraint and careful of points
of dignity and precedence. The presence of a king was
of some help, the presence of two only made matters
worse. If the causes of rivalry at home and the slighting
of Philip's sister could have been forgotten, there was still
the fact that Richard was Philip's vassal as well as his
equal, and Richard was not of the type to spare Philip's
susceptibilities. Rich, open-handed, fond of display,

Lion-Heart "loved the lime-light," and his overbearing nature and lack of tact made it impossible for him to coöperate with others. He characteristically went his own way, paying scant attention to Philip and acting as if the leadership of the expedition belonged to himself as a matter of course. Relations became strained during the sojourn at Messina and grew worse in Palestine, where the affairs of the Latin kingdom and the rivalries of lesser princes added fuel to the flame. "The two kings and peoples," says an English chronicler, "did less together than they would have done separately, and each set but light store by the other." Sick of the whole enterprise, after four months in the East, Philip seized the first excuse to return home, departing in August, 1191.

Richard stayed a year longer in Palestine, yet he never entered Jerusalem and had finally to retire with a disappointing truce and to spend another year, and more, languishing in German prisons. The events of these months do not concern the history of Normandy, but if we would behold Richard in his fairest light we must see him as he rushed to the relief of Joppa on the first of August, 1192, wading ashore from his red galley with the cry, "Perish the man who would hang back," covering the landing of his followers with his crossbow, making his way by a winding stair to the house of the Templars on the town wall, and then, sword in hand, clearing the town of three thousand Turks and pursuing them into the plain with but three horsemen; or, four days later, repelling a Mameluke attack in force by a most skilful tactical arrangement of his meagre army, directing the battle on the beach while he also kept the town clear, "slaying innumerable Turks with his gleaming sword, here cleaving a man from the crown of his head to his teeth," there cutting off with one blow the head, shoulder, and right arm of a Saracen emir, his coat of mail and his horse bristling with javelins and arrows like a hedgehog, yet "remaining unconquerable and unwounded in accordance with the divine decree." [1]

What most concerned the Norman empire was the king's absence since the summer of 1190, prolonged by his captivity in Germany until the spring of 1194. Although Philip had taken an oath before leaving Palestine to respect Richard's men and possessions during his absence, and even to protect them like his own city of Paris, he sought release from this engagement as soon as he reached Rome on his homeward journey, and once back in France he soon began active preparations for an attack on the Plantagenet territories. With Richard safe in a German dungeon, he seized a large part of the Norman border and made a secret treaty with John which secured the surrender of all the lands east of the Seine and important fortresses in Anjou and Touraine. He offered huge sums of money to secure Richard's custody

[1] See the extracts from the chroniclers translated in T. A. Archer, *The Crusade of Richard I* (London, 1888), pp. 285 *ff*.

or even his continued detention in Germany, and when early in 1194 he warned John that "the Devil was loose" at last, he was besieging the great fortress of Verneuil on the Norman frontier.  When Richard landed at Barfleur in May, amid the ringing of bells and processions singing "God has come again in his strength," it is small wonder that he came breathing vengeance and slaughter, and that the rest of his life is a record of scarcely interrupted war against the king of France.  For many years he is said to have refused the sacrament lest he might have to forgive his enemy.  Again and again he had Philip on the run.  Once Philip lost all his baggage and saved himself by turning aside to hear mass while Richard rode by; on another occasion Richard drove the French into Gisors so that the bridge broke under them "and the king of France drank of the river, and twenty of his knights were drowned."

Such scenes, however, are only the striking episodes in a series of campaigns which are confused and complicated and do not lend themselves to clear narration. Decisive engagements were rare, each side seeking rather to wear out the other.  Money was spent freely for allies and mercenaries — a contemporary called the struggle one between the pound sterling and the pound of Tours, and the advantage was on the side of the pounds sterling by reason of their greater number. There was usually a campaign in the spring and summer, ending in a truce in the autumn which the church tried to prolong into a lasting peace but which soon broke down in a new war. The wars were for the most part border forays, in which the country was burned and wasted far and wide, to the injury chiefly of the peasants, upon whom the burden of mediæval warfare mainly fell. "First destroy the land, then the enemy," was the watchword. Booty and ransom were the object as well as military advantages, so that even the contests between knights had their sordid side, so definitely were they directed toward taking profitable prisoners; while feudal notions of honor might cause Richard to put out the eyes of fifteen prisoners and send them to Philip under the guidance of one of their number who had been left one eye, whereupon Philip blinded an equal number of knights and sent them to Richard under the guidance of the wife of one of them, "in order," says his eulogist,[1] "that no one should think he was afraid of Richard or inferior to him in force and courage."

The brunt of the war fell on Normandy and ultimately on the castles which supplied the duchy's lack of natural frontiers. To supplement the great interior fortresses of Caen, Falaise, Argentan, Montfort, and Rouen, Henry I began the organization of a series of fortifications on the southern and eastern borders. Henry II, we are told, improved or renewed nearly all these strongholds, and especially Gisors, the frontier gateway toward France, on which fortress the exchequer

---

[1] Guillaume le Breton, *Philippide*, v, lines 316–27.

roll shows him expending 2650 pounds Angevin in a single year. These castles, remains of many of which are still standing, were typical of the best military architecture of their age, but they were inferior in strength and scientific construction to the great fortresses of Christian Syria, such as Krak or Margat, which seem to have gone back to Byzantine and even Persian models. A keen warrior like Richard had not spent his two years in Palestine without gaining an expert knowledge of eastern methods in the art of war, and we are not surprised to find that he had Saracen soldiers and Syrian artillerymen with him in his Norman campaigns, and that he made large use of oriental experience in strengthening his defences. His masterpiece, of course, was Château Gaillard, the saucy castle on the Seine controlling the passage of the river and its tributaries in that region of the Norman Vexin which was the great bone of contention between the Plantagenets and the French kings. Having first expropriated at great expense the lord of the region, the archbishop of Rouen, he fortified the adjacent island of Andeli and laid out a new town on the bank. This he surrounded with water and rëenforced with towers and battlements, protecting the whole with a stockade across the river and outlying works farther up. Then on the great rock above he built the fortress, with its triangular advance work, its elliptical citadel, and its circular keep surrounded by a "*fossé* cut almost vertically out of the rock." There was no dead angle, such as permitted sappers to reach the base of rectilinear walls, but instead a sloping base down which projectiles might ricochet; nor was there, as at the corners of square towers, any part of the surrounding area which could not be reached by direct fire from within. "The approaches and the *fossé*," says Dieulafoy,[1] "were covered by the fire of the garrison right up to the foot of the scarp, and no sapper could touch any point in towers or walls, provided that the fortress was under the direction of an experienced commander." This qualification is important, for the new type of fortification was designed for an active defence, one might almost say an offensive defence, and not for the mere passive resistance with which the older strategy had been content. The works at Andeli, carried on largely under Richard's personal direction, occupied more than a year of labor and cost nearly 50,000 pounds Angevin, which we find distributed in the royal accounts over lumber and stone and hardware, and among masons and carpenters and stone-cutters and lesser laborers.

By the year 1199 Richard had recovered his Norman possessions save Gisors and certain castles on the border, where Philip never lost his foothold, and he had raised an effective barrier to French advance in the valley of the Seine. Strong allies were on his side, and the diplomatic situation was decidedly in his favor. Never had

---

[1] *Le Château-Gaillard*, in *Mémoires de l'Académie des Inscriptions*, XXXVI, 1, p. 330.

Philip been so hard pressed, and even the friendly legate of the Pope could secure for him nothing better than the retention of Gisors in the truce which was then drawn up. And then a second stroke of fortune, greater even than the captivity of 1192, came to Philip's aid. Richard, impetuous and headstrong as ever, spoiled all by a raid on an Aquitanian rebel in which he lost his life. His energy, his military skill, and his vivid personality had concealed the fundamental weakness of his position against France; his removal meant the swift fall of the Norman empire.

At Richard's death there were two possible successors, his younger brother John, whom he had designated heir, and his nephew Arthur, son of his elder brother Geoffrey and duke of Brittany. There was enough uncertainty in feudal law to admit of a plausible case for either one, but Arthur was only twelve and John quickly took possession, being crowned at Rouen in April and at Westminster in May. Arthur, however, had the following of his Bretons and, what was more important, the support of Philip Augustus, who used Arthur against John as he had used John against Richard and Richard against his father. Philip confirmed Arthur as count of Anjou, Maine, and Touraine, and soon brought him to Paris, where he was betrothed to Philip's daughter. Nevertheless the course of events at first favored John. Philip was in the midst of the great struggle with Pope

Innocent III over the divorce of his queen Ingeborg, and a treaty was signed in 1200, by which, on giving up territory in the Norman border and in central France and paying a large relief of 20,000 marks for his lands, John was confirmed in his control of Anjou and Brittany, while a visit to Paris, where he was splendidly received, seemed to crown the reconciliation. In a position, however, where all possible strength and resourcefulness were required, John's defects of character proved fatal. No one could depend upon him for loyalty, judgment, or even persistence, and he quickly earned his name of "Soft-Sword."

Meanwhile the legally-minded Philip, while spending money freely on John's followers and abating nothing of his diplomatic and military efforts, brought to bear the weapons of law. The revival of legal studies in the twelfth century had given rise in western Europe to a body of professional lawyers, skilled in the Roman and the canon law, and quick to turn their learning to the advantage of the princes whom they served. Philip had a number of such advisers at his court, and they doubtless contributed to the more lawyerlike methods of doing things which make their appearance in his reign; but it was feudal custom, and not Roman law, that he used against John. In law John was Philip's vassal, — indeed, he had just confessed as much in the treaty of 1200, — and as such was held to attend Philip's feudal court and subject himself to its decision in disputes with other vassals. It might be urged that the king of England was too great a man to submit to such jurisdiction, and that the duke of Normandy had been in the habit of satisfying his feudal obligations by a formal ceremony at the Norman frontier; still the technical law was on the side of the king of France, and a suzerain had at last come who was able to translate theory into fact. In the course of a series of adventures in Poitou John carried off the fiancée of one of his barons of the house of Lusignan, who appealed to his superior lord, the king of France. All this was in due form, but Philip was no lion of justice eager to redress injuries for justice' sake. He waited nearly two years, John's visit to Paris falling in the interval, and then, when he was ready to execute sentence, promptly summoned John before the feudal court of peers. John neither came nor appeared through a representative, and the court in April, 1202, declared him deprived of all his lands for having refused to obey his lord's commands or render the services due from him as vassal. The capture of Arthur temporarily checked Philip; the boy's murder by John in the course of 1203 simply recoiled on the murderer. Whether this crime led to a second condemnation by the court of peers, as was alleged by the French at the time of the abortive invasion of England in 1216, is a question which has been sharply discussed among scholars. What has now become the orthodox view holds that there was no second condemnation, but a clever case has recently been made by Powicke, who, minimizing the importance of the accepted argument from the silence of immediate contemporaries, argues, on the basis of the *Annals of Margam*, that there probably was a second condemnation in 1204. After all, the question is of subordinate importance, for Philip's effective action was based on the trial of 1202, and by 1204 John's fate was already sealed.

The decisive point in the campaign against Normandy was the capture of Château Gaillard, the key to the Seine valley, in May, 1204, after a siege of six months which seems to have justified its designer, save for a stone bridge which sheltered the engineers who undermined the outer wall. Western Normandy fell before an attack from the side of Brittany; the great fortresses of the centre, Argentan, Falaise, and Caen, opened their gates to Philip; and with the surrender of Rouen, 24 June, 1204, Philip was master of Normandy. John had lingered in England, doing nothing to support the defense, and when he crossed at last in 1206 he was obliged to sign a final surrender of all the territories north of the Loire, retaining only southern Poitou and Gascony. Gascony and England were united for two centuries longer, but the only connection was by sea. The control of the Seine and the Loire had been lost, and with that passed away the Plantagenet empire.

The results of the separation of Normandy from

England have been a favorite subject with historians, and especially with those who approach the Middle Ages from the point of view of modern politics and modern ideas of nationality. It all seems so natural that Normandy should belong with France and not with England. Nationality, however, is an elusive thing, and many forces besides geography have made the modern map. England in the Middle Ages had much more in common with Normandy than she had with Wales or Scotland, while in feeling, as well as in space, the Irish Sea was wider than the Channel. From the English point of view there was nothing inevitable in the loss of Normandy. On the French side the matter is more obvious. If Paris was to be the capital, it must control the Seine and the Loire, and when it gained control of them, its position in France was assured. The possession of Normandy meant far more to France than to England. Moreover the conquest of Normandy cut England and France loose from each other. The Anglo-Norman barons must decide whether they would serve the king of England or the king of France, and they were quickly absorbed into the country with which they threw in their lot. It was no longer possible to play one set of interests against another; turned back on themselves, the English barons met John on their own ground and won the Great Charter, so that the loss of Normandy has a direct bearing on the growth of English liberty. "When the Normans became French," concludes Powicke, "they did a great deal more than bring their national epic to a close. They permitted the English once more to become a nation, and they established the French state for all time." [1]

Viewed in this way, the end of Normandy almost seems more glorious than Normandy itself; as was said of Samson, "the dead which he slew at his death were more than they which he slew in his life." But of course in the larger sense the work of the Norman empire was not ended in 1204. For one thing, the administrative organization of the Norman duchy could not fail to exert an influence upon the French monarchy. In spite of the great progress made by the Capetian kings of the twelfth century, the Norman government still maintained its marked superiority as a system of judicial and fiscal administration, and Philip Augustus was not the man to neglect the lessons it might have for him. The nature and extent of Norman influence upon French institutions is a subject which is still dark to us and for lack of evidence may always remain dark; but there can be little doubt that Norman precedents were followed at various points in the development of the Parlement of Paris and in the elaboration of the French financial system. In the main, however, the influence was inevitably in the other direction, from France upon Normandy, not from Normandy upon

[1] *The Loss of Normandy*, p. 449.

France. There was, it is true, no sudden change. Philip respected vested interests, both in the church and among the barons, and preserved Norman customs, so that the duchy long retained its individuality of law, of local organization, and of character, and secured its rights from Louis X in a document of 1315, the *Charte aux Normands*, which has sometimes been compared in a small way to the Great Charter. The *Coutume de Normandie* persisted, like the customs of the other great provinces, until the French Revolution, but it was a body of custom worked out under the influence of the central government and gradually absorbing the jurisprudence of the king's court. If the Norman exchequer continued to sit at Rouen, it was presided over by commissioners sent out from Paris. Even that most characteristic of Norman institutions, trial by jury, was insensibly modified by the new inquisitorial procedure of the thirteenth century and silently disappeared from the practice of the Continent. As in law and government, so in culture and social life, the forces of centralization did their work none the less effectively because they were gradual, and Normandy became a part of France.

There was, it is true, a period when Normandy was once more united to England, this time as a conquered country. Between 1417 and 1419 Henry V subdued Normandy in a series of well-conducted campaigns, and he and his son remained in possession of the duchy until 1450. During this period of English rule no effort seems to have been made to restore earlier conditions which had now been outgrown: law, local government, fiscal organization continued unchanged. English officials were, of course, appointed, and English immigration was encouraged at the expense of the lands of the Normans who had left the province. The first Norman university was founded at Caen in the reign of Henry VI. In the face, however, of all efforts at conciliation and fair treatment the population remained hostile. The idea that the Englishman was a foreigner had grown up during two centuries of absence; it was to crystallize definitely as the conception of French nationality took form through the work of Joan of Arc. Lavisse has reminded us [1] that this war "was not a conflict between one nation and another, between the genius of one people and that of another; nevertheless it continued, and was fierce as well as long. From year to year the hatred against the English increased. In contact with the foreigner France began to know herself, like the *ego* in contact with the *non-ego*. Vanquished she felt the disgrace of defeat. Acts of municipal and local patriotism preceded and heralded French patriotism, which finally blossomed out in Joan of Arc, and sanctified itself with the perfume of a miracle. Out of France with the English! They left France, and France

[1] *General View of the Political History of Europe* (translated by Charles Gross), p. 64.

came into existence." In this rapid growth of French national consciousness Normandy had its full share, and some of its great scenes are set on Norman soil. It was at Rouen that Joan of Arc was tried and condemned by the Inquisition; it was in the old market-place of this same city that the English soldiers discovered too late that they had burned a saint.

And so it came about that twenty years later the Normans welcomed the troops of Charles VII and passed finally under French sway. Proud of its past, proud also of its provincialisms and local peculiarities, Normandy was nevertheless French in feeling and interests, and grew more French with time under the unifying force of the absolute monarchy, the Revolution, and the modern republic. It ceased to be a duchy in 1467; it ceased to be even a political division with the creation of the modern departments in 1790. Its last survival as an area recognized by the government, the ecclesiastical province of Rouen, disappeared with the final separation of church and state in 1905. The only unity which its five departments now retain is that of the history and tradition of a common past — of a *petite patrie* now swallowed up in the nation.

Only at one point did the old Normandy really maintain itself against the forces of centralization, namely in the Channel Islands, those "bits of France fallen into the sea and picked up by England," as Victor Hugo calls them. These were not conquered by Philip or his successors, and have remained from that day to this attached to the English crown. They still have their *baillis* and *vicomtes*, their knights' fees and feudal modes of tenure. The Norman dialect is still their language; the *Coutume de Normandie* is still the basis of their law; and one may still hear, in disputes concerning property in Jersey and Guernsey, the old cry of *haro* which preserves one of the most archaic features of Norman procedure.

After all is said, it is in England that the most permanent work of the Normans survives. They created the English central government and impressed upon it their conceptions of order and of law. Their feudalism permeated English society; their customs shaped much of English jurisprudence; their kings and nobles were the dominant class in English government. Freeman could never understand those who claimed that, as he declared, "we English are not ourselves but somebody else." The fact, however, remains that in a mixed race — and all races are to some extent mixed — there is no such thing as 'ourselves'; and if the numerical preponderance in the English people is largely that of pre-Norman elements, the Norman strain has exerted an influence out of all proportion to its numerical strength. Without William the Conqueror and Henry II the English would not be 'themselves,' whatever else they might have become.

For a more specific illustration let us come back once more to the jury. If the jury died out in Normandy, it survived in England, where it flourished in the fertile soil of the popular local courts. It spread to the British colonies and to the United States; it has in recent times been reintroduced on the Continent. But it is still the same fundamental institution, bound by direct continuity with the old Frankish procedure through the Norman inquests of the twelfth century. Wherever the twelve good men and true are gathered together, we can see the juries of Henry II behind them. In such matters the Norman influence is thus as wide as the common law; we are all heirs of the early Normans. As Freeman well says: "We can never be as if the Norman had never come among us. We ever bear about us the signs of his presence. Our colonists have carried those signs with them into distant lands, to remind men that settlers in America and Australia came from a land which the Norman once entered as a conqueror." [1]

Our survey of Norman history might perhaps stop here; but it needs to be rounded out in two directions. We have been so busy with the external history of the Norman empire and with the constitutional developments to which it gave rise, that we have had no time to examine the society and culture of Normandy in its flourishing period of imperialism. And we have been

[1] *William the Conqueror*, p. 2.

concentrating our attention so exclusively on the dominions of the Plantagenets that we have left out of view that greater Normandy to the south which constitutes one of the most brilliant chapters of Norman achievement and one of the most fascinating subjects of European history. These topics will be the themes of the three remaining lectures.

## BIBLIOGRAPHICAL NOTE

The best account of the downfall of the Norman empire is Powicke, *The Loss of Normandy*, where abundant references will be found to further material. The general narratives of Adams, Davis, and Ramsay may also be consulted, as well as Miss Norgate, *John Lackland* (London, 1902). For the French side see Luchaire, in Lavisse, *Histoire de France*, III, 1. The fullest treatment of relations between the Plantagenets and France, down to 1199, is A. Cartellieri, *Philipp II. August* (Leipzig, 1899–1910), supplemented by his *Richard Löwenherz im heiligen Lande*, in *Historische Zeitschrift*, CI, pp. 1–27 (1908), and *Philipp II. August und der Zusammenbruch des angiovinischen Reiches* (Leipzig, 1913). For the controversy concerning John's condemnation by the court of Philip, see Gross, *Sources and Literature*, nos. 2829, 2833. Characterizations of Richard and John by Stubbs will be found in his *Historical Introductions*, pp. 315 ff., 439 ff. J. Lehmann, *Johann ohne Land* (Berlin, 1904), is more favorable to John. The biography of the Young King is traced by P. C. E. Hodgson, *Jung Heinrich, König von England* (Jena, 1906).

There is no general work on the English occupation of Normandy in the fifteenth century; the scattered monographs are mentioned in Prentout, *La Normandie*, pp. 71–76. Something may be expected from the continuation of the late J. H. Wylie's work on the reign of Henry V.

# VI

IN turning from the general course of Norman history in the eleventh and twelfth centuries to examine Norman life and culture in this period, we encounter the difficulties inherent in any attempt to cut a cross-section of human society in an age which was not conscious of being a society and has left us for the description of itself only raw materials of a fragmentary and uneven sort. The chroniclers confine themselves almost entirely to external events, the charters deal chiefly with land and boundaries and rights over the land, much of the literature is theological commentary or rhetorical commonplace which reflects nothing of the age in which it was written; what is lacking in all is the concrete detail of daily life from which alone social and economic conditions and even government itself can be understood. And when we have pieced together as best we may some notions of Normandy in this period, our knowledge of the parallel conditions in other regions is often so inadequate that we cannot be certain how far our results are characteristic of Normandy, how far typical of the time, or, because of the scattered nature of our material, how far they may be merely individual and isolated. Much of the social history of the Middle Ages is still unwritten; for lack of evidence much can never be written. Until the available sources have been more fully explored, nothing beyond a provisional sketch can be attempted.

Fortunately for our purposes, the fundamental structure of society in the earlier Middle Ages was exceedingly simple. There were three classes, those who fought, those who labored, and those who prayed, corresponding respectively to the nobles, the peasants, and the clergy. Created by the simple needs of the feudal age, this primitive division of labor was even declared an institution of divine origin and necessary to the harmonious life of man. It seemed right and natural that the nobles should defend the country and maintain order, the clergy lead men to salvation, the peasants support by their labor these two beneficent classes, as well as themselves. As an ideal of social organization, this system of classes is open to obvious objections, not the least of which is the persistent killing and plundering of the peasants by the class whose function it was to protect and defend them; but as a description of actual conditions, it expresses very well the facts of the case.

With respect to the fighting class, it is characteristic of the Norman habit of order and organization that the military service of the nobles was early defined with more system and exactness in Normandy than in the neighboring countries of northern France. We have already seen that at a period well before 1066 the amount of service due from the great lords to the duke had been fixed in rough units of five or multiples of five, and these again subdivided among their vassals and attached to specific pieces of land which were hence called knights' fees, an arrangement which the Normans carried to England and probably to Sicily as well. By 1172, when a comprehensive list was first drawn up, subinfeudation had produced about 1500 knights' fees in Normandy, the largest holders being the bishop of Bayeux and the earl of Leicester with 120, the count of Ponthieu with 111, and Earl Giffard with 103. From these the class of fully armed knights reached down to the holders of small fractions of a knight's fee, all however serving with the full armor which in course of time came to mark them off as nobles from the vavassors, or free soldiers, whose equipment was less complete and whose service tended to take the form of castle guard and similar duties. Quite early also custom had defined other characteristic features of the feudal service in Normandy, such as the period of forty days, the limitation of the obligation to the frontiers of the duchy, and the incidents of wardship and marriage, deductions from feudal principles which were here carried to their logical conclusions.

The symbol of the authority of the military class, the outward and visible sign of feudalism, was the castle, where the lord resided and from which he exercised his authority over his fief. Originating in the period of anarchy which accompanied the dissolution of the Frankish empire and the invasions of the ninth and tenth centuries, the castle spread over northern France as feudalism spread, and was introduced into England by the Normans when they here established their feudal state. The earliest castles of Normandy and of England were not, however, the massive stone donjons which Freeman peopled with devils and evil men. With some exceptions, of which the Tower of London is the most noteworthy, these 'hateful structures' were built of wood and surrounded by a stockade, surmounting an artificial mound, or *motte*, thrown up from the deep moat at its base. A great drawbridge, cleated so that horses should not slip on the steep incline, led from the farther side of the moat directly to the second story of the tower, of which the ground floor, used only for stores and the custody of prisoners, had no entrance from without. Fortresses of this type have naturally left nothing behind them save the outlines of their mounds and moats, but they are well known from contemporary descriptions and are clearly discernible in the Bayeux Tapestry, which gives rude pictures of the strongholds of Dol, Rennes, Dinan, and Bayeux, and shows a stockaded mound in actual process of construction at Hastings. The heavy timbers of these lofty block-houses offered stout resistance to battering rams, but they were always in great danger from fire, and wood was replaced by stone in the course of the twelfth century, to which belong the 'stern square towers' which still survive in Normandy and England, as well as the earliest examples of the more defensible round keeps and square keeps flanked with round towers. Whether of wood or stone, the donjon was a stern place, built for strength rather than for comfort, and bending the life of those within it to the imperious necessities of defence. Space was at a premium, windows were few and small, — sometimes only a single window and a single room to each story, — trap-doors and ladders often did the work of stairways, and from the wooden castles fires were usually excluded. Nevertheless the donjons were not, as was once supposed, mere "towers of refuge used only in time of war," but "were the permanent residences of the nobles of the eleventh and twelfth centuries." [1] Only toward the close of this period do the outer buildings develop, so as to give something of the room and convenience demanded by the rising standard of comfort; only in the thirteenth century do the more spacious castles without keeps begin to make their appearance.

It is significant of the progress made by the ducal authority in Normandy that by the time of William the Conqueror definite restrictions had been placed upon the creation of these strongholds of local power and resistance. Except with the duke's license no one could build a castle, or erect a fortress on a rock or an island,

[1] Armitage, *Early Norman Castles of the British Isles*, p. 359.

or even dig a fosse in the open country so deep that the earth could not be thrown out from the bottom without artificial aid, while palisades were required to be built in a simple line and without alures or special works of defence. When the duke desired, he might also place garrisons in his barons' castles and demand hostages for their loyalty. These principles, which were applied also in England, were of course often difficult to enforce, and they were supplemented in the twelfth century by the development of a great system of ducal castles, secured partly by enlarging and strengthening the older fortresses of Rouen, Caen, Falaise, and Argentan, partly, as we have already seen, by new strongholds on the frontiers. Powicke has shown us how these castles became the chief administrative centres in the reigns of Henry II and Richard, and how the royal letters and accounts reveal their many-sided activity in the busy days of peace as well as in the more strenuous times of war.[1] Under *châtelains* who were royal officers rather than feudal vassals, with garrisons of mercenaries and retinues of knights and serjeants, clerks and chaplains and personal servants, they foreshadow the ultimate replacement of baronial donjons by a royal bureaucracy.

It is doubtless because of the dominant position of the duke that Normandy is less rich than some other parts of France in picturesque types of feudal lords or vivid episodes of feudal conflicts. When they go beyond the

[1] *The Loss of Normandy*, pp. 298 ff.

affairs of the church, the Norman chroniclers are prone to concentrate their attention upon the deeds of the ducal house, and their accounts of the great vassals tend to be dry and genealogical. The chief exception is Ordericus Vitalis, whose theme and geographical position lead him to treat at length the long anarchy under Robert Curthose and the incessant conflicts of the great lords his neighbors on the southern border, the houses of Bellême, Grentemaisnil, Conches, and Breteuil. In the main it is a dreary tale of surprises and sieges, of treachery and captivity and sudden death, relieved from time to time by brighter episodes — the lady Isabel of Conches sitting in the great hall as the young men of the castle tell their dreams; the daily battle for bread around the oven at the siege of Courcy; the table spread and the pots seething on the coals for the lord and lady of Saint-Céneri who never came back; the man of Saint-Évroul who, by the saint's aid, walks unharmed out of custody at Domfront; the marvellous vision of the army of knights and ladies in torment which appeared to the priest of Bonneval.

With these episodes of Norman feudalism it is interesting to compare the picture of Anglo-Norman society a hundred years later which we find in that unique piece of feudal biography, the *History of William the Marshal.* Companion to the Young King and witness of the final shame of Henry II, pilgrim to Jerusalem and Cologne, advanced to positions of trust under Richard and John, earl of Striguil and Pembroke and regent of England under Henry III, the Earl Marshal stood in close relations to the chief men and movements of his day. His biographer, however, does not let himself wander to tell of others' deeds, and while his work contains material of much importance for the general history of the time, its chief value lies in its reflection of the life of the age and its faithful portrait of the man himself — soldier of fortune, gentleman-adventurer if you will, but always loyal, honorable, straightforward, and true, by the standards of his time a man without fear and without reproach. Brought up in the Norman castle of Tancarville, the Marshal, like the Young King his master, became passionately addicted to tournaments, *par éminence* the knightly sport of the Middle Ages, which made hunting and other pastimes seem tame and furnished the best preparation for real war, since, as an English chronicler tells us, in order to shine in war a knight "must have seen his own blood flow, have had his jaw crack under the blow of his adversary, have been dashed to the earth with such force as to feel the weight of his foe, and unhorsed twenty times he must twenty times have retrieved his failures, more set than ever on the combat." Unknown to England before the reign of Richard, these manly sports flourished most of all in France, the country of chivalry and feats of arms, and for several years we follow the Marshal from combat to combat through Normandy and Maine, Champagne

and the Ile-de-France, so that his renown spread from
Poitou to the Rhine. At one period in his life he tour-
neyed every fortnight. The tournaments of his day,
however, were not the elegant and fashionable affairs of
the fourteenth and fifteenth centuries which the word is
apt to call to our minds, assemblages of beauty as well
as of prowess, held in special enclosures before crowded
galleries, with elaborate rules respecting armor and
weapons and the conditions of conflict. On the contrary,
they were fought like battles, in the open, with all the
arms and methods of war and all its manœuvres and
ferocity of attack; indeed they differed from war mainly
in being voluntary and limited to a single day. After one
series of such thunderous encounters the Marshal was
found in a smithy, his head on the anvil and the smith
working with hammer and pincers to remove his bat-
tered helmet. In a great tournament at Lagni three
thousand knights are said to have been engaged, of
which the Young King furnished eighty. Knights
fought for honor and fame and for sheer joy of combat;
they fought also, we must remember, for the horses and
armor and ransoms of the captives. In a Norman tournament the Marshal captured ten knights and twelve
horses. Between Pentecost and Lent of one year their
clerks calculated that he and his companion had taken
prisoners three hundred knights, without counting
horses and harness; yet he seems to have preserved the
golden mean between the careless *largesse* of the Young

King and the merely mercenary motives of the large number who frequented tournaments for the sake of gain.

Concerning the great agricultural class upon which the whole social system rested, our information is of a scattered and uneven sort. The man with the hoe did not interest the mediæval chronicler, and he did not gain a voice of his own in the period which we have under review. The annals of the time are indeed careful to record the drouths and floods, the seasons of plague, pestilence, and famine of which Normandy seems to have had its share, but they tell us nothing of the effects of these evils upon the class which they most directly concerned; while the charters, leases, and manorial records from which our knowledge of the peasants must be built up give us in this period isolated and unrelated facts. Moreover our information is confined almost entirely to the lands of churches and monasteries, where agriculture was likely to be more progressive because of their closer relations to the world outside. Normandy was a fertile country, and, so far as we can judge, its agricultural population fared well as compared with that of other regions. Certainly there is here, after the eleventh century, no trace of serfdom or the freeing of serfs, and the free position of its farming class distinguished the duchy from most of the lands of northern France. In other respects it is hard to discern important differences between the Norman peasants and those of other regions. After the suppression of an insurrection at the beginning of this century, we do not hear of any general rising of the Norman peasants, parallel to those risings which make a sad and futile chapter in the annals of many parts of Europe in the Middle Ages. It was, however, a local revolt of the thirteenth century on the lands of the monks of Mont-Saint-Michel that brought out one of the best descriptions of life on a Norman manor, the *Conte des Vilains de Verson*,[1] and, while it is a bit late for our purpose, it is confirmed by documentary evidence, and may well serve as an illustration of the obligations of the agricultural class: —

In June the peasants must cut and pile the hay and carry it to the manor house. In August they must reap and carry in the convent's grain; their own grain lies exposed to wind and rain while they hunt out the assessor of the *champart* and carry his share to his barn. On the Nativity of the Virgin the villain owes the pork-due, one pig in eight; at St. Denis' day the *cens;* at Christmas the fowl, fine and good, and thereafter the grain-due of two *sétiers* of barley and three quarters of wheat; on Palm Sunday the sheep-due; at Easter he must plow, sow and harrow. When there is building the tenant must bring stone and serve the masons; he must also haul the convent's wood for two *deniers* a day. If he sells his land, he owes the lord a thirteenth of its value; if he marries his daughter outside the seigniory, he pays a fine. He must grind his grain at the seigniorial mill and bake his bread at the seigniorial oven, where the customary charges do not satisfy the attendants, who grumble and threaten to leave his bread unbaked.

[1] Printed by Delisle, *Études sur la classe agricole*, pp. 668 *ff*.

So long as mediæval society remained almost entirely agricultural there was no need of adapting its organization to other classes than those which have just been described. In course of time, however, the growth of industry and commerce, very slow before the eleventh century, but rapid and constant in the period during and after the Crusades, as may be seen by the large number of markets and fairs in Normandy, created a new class of dwellers in towns who demanded recognition of their peculiar character and status. By reason of the nature of their occupations they sought release from the seigniorial system, with its forced labor, its frequent payments, and its vexatious restrictions upon freedom of movement and freedom of buying and selling; and as their economic needs drew them together into industrial and commercial centres of population, they developed a collective feeling and demanded collective treatment. They asked, not, as has sometimes been said, for the overthrow of the feudal system, but for a place within it which should recognize their peculiar economic and political interests; and the result of their efforts, when fully successful, was to form what has been called a collective seigniory, standing as a body in the relation of vassal to lord or king, and owing the obligations of homage, fealty, and communal military service. But while not anti-feudal in theory, this movement was often anti-feudal in practice, so far at least as the rights and privileges of the immediate overlord were concerned, and it led to friction and often to armed contests with bishop, baron, or king. In Normandy, significantly, we find none of those communal revolts which meet us throughout the north of France and even as near as LeMans; the towns are always subject to the ultimate authority of the duke, whose domanial rights were considerable even in the episcopal cities and who favored those forms of urban development which strengthened the military resources of the duchy. The early history of the Norman towns is one of the most obscure chapters in Norman history, but it indicates a variety of influences which do not fit into any one of the many theories of municipal origins which have been the subject of so much learned controversy. Some towns were originally fortified places, like the baronial stronghold of Breteuil or Henry I's fortresses of Verneuil, Nonancourt, and Pontorson on the southern border. Some took advantage of the protection of a monastery, as in the case of Fécamp or the *bourgs* of the abbot and abbess of Caen. The great ports, like Barfleur and Dieppe, obviously owed their importance to trade, and it was trade which created the prosperity of the chief towns of the duchy, Rouen and Caen. However developed, the Norman municipal type exerted no small influence upon urban organization: the laws of Breteuil became the model for Norman foundations on the Welsh border and in Ireland; the *Établissements* of Rouen were copied in the principal towns of western France, — Tours and Poitiers, Angoulême and

La Rochelle, even to Gascon Bayonne on the Spanish frontier.

If we take as an illustration of this development the principal Norman town, Rouen, we find no evidence regarding its institutions before the twelfth century, while its organization as a commune dates from the reign of Henry II and probably from the year 1171. The fundamental law, or *Établissements*, which Rouen then received and which became the model for communal government elsewhere in Normandy, constitutes a body of one hundred peers who meet once a fortnight for judicial and other business and who choose from their number each year the twelve *échevins*, or magistrates, and the twelve councillors who sit with the *échevins* to form the council of *jurés*. Besides these boards, which are typical of mediæval town constitutions, the peers also nominate three candidates for the office of mayor, but the choice among these is made by the king, and the greater authority of the mayor in this system is evidently designed to secure more effective royal control. It is the mayor who leads the communal militia, receives the revenues, supervises the execution of sentences, and presides over all meetings of magistrates and boards. The administration of justice through its own magistrates is perhaps the most valued privilege of the commune, but the gravest crimes are reserved for the cognizance of royal officers, and the presence of the king or a session of his assize is sufficient to suspend all communal powers of justice. In a state like the Norman the limits of municipal self-government are clear.

The importance of Rouen as a commercial and industrial centre was not, however, dependent upon its form of government. Its ancient gild of cordwainers had been recognized by Henry I and Stephen, its trading privileges were confirmed in one of the earliest charters of Henry II. Save for a single ship yearly from Cherbourg, the merchants of Rouen had a monopoly of trade with Ireland; in England they could go through all the markets of the land; in London they were quit of all payments save for wine and great fish and had exclusive rights in their special wharf of Dowgate. Later in Henry's reign they were even freed of all dues throughout his dominions. Only a citizen might take a shipload of merchandise past Rouen or bring wine to a cellar in the town. Besides the great trade in wine we hear of dealings in leather, cloth, grain, and especially salt and salt fish. Under Henry II the ducal rights over the town were worth annually more than 3,000 *livres*. Apart from their share in this general prosperity, the citizens had special exemptions in the matter of duties and tolls on goods which they brought in, while the freedom from feudal restraints which characterized all burgage tenures put a premium upon their holding of property. Besides the privileged areas belonging to the cathedral and the neighboring abbeys, a foothold in the city was valued by others: the bishop of Bayeux had a town house; the abbot of Caen prized a cellar and an exemption from wine-dues which he owed to the generosity of William the Conqueror; the clerks and chaplains of the king's household took advantage of their opportunities to acquire rents and houses at Rouen, as well as at London and Winchester.

Unfortunately no one has left us in this period a description of the busy life of Rouen such as Fitz Stephen has given of contemporary London, and it is only with the imagination that we can bring before our eyes the ships at their wharves with their bales of marten-skins from Ireland and casks of wine from Burgundy and the south, the fullers and dyers, millers and tanners plying their trades along the Eau de Robec, the burgesses trafficking in the streets and the cathedral close, the royal clerks and serjeants hastening on their master's business. Still more to be regretted is the disappearance of those material remains of its ancient splendor which until the last century retained the form and flavor, if not the actual wood and stone, of the mediæval city. To-day scarcely anything survives above ground of the Rouen of the dukes — of its walls and gates, destroyed by Philip Augustus, of the castle by the river, with the tower from which Henry I threw the traitor Conan and the great hall and rooms renewed by his grandson, of the stone bridge of the Empress Matilda, of the royal park and palace across the Seine at Quevilly. Only the great St. Romain's tower of the cathedral and an early bit of the abbey-church of Saint-Ouen still body forth the un-broken continuity of the Norman past.

The Norman church throughout the period of our study stands in the closest relation to the general condi-tions of Norman society. The monasteries and churches of the region had been almost completely wiped out by the northern invasions, and while the Northmen soon adopted the religion of their new neighbors, it was many years before ecclesiastical life and discipline again reached the level of the other dioceses of France. As late as the year 1001 a Burgundian monk reported that there was hardly a priest in Normandy who could read the lessons or say his psalms correctly. The prelates led the life of the great feudal families of which they were members, distributing the property of the church as fiefs to their friends or gifts to their numerous progeny; and the lower clergy, for the most part married, sought to pass on their benefices to their children. In the course of the eleventh century, however, more canonical stand-ards began to prevail, largely through the influence of the monks of Cluny. Older foundations like Fécamp were renewed, and the Norman lords soon began to vie with one another in the endowment of new monastic establishments. To the half-century which preceded the Conquest of England we can trace the beginnings of twenty important monasteries and six nunneries, not counting priories and smaller foundations, a movement for which contemporaries could find no parallel short of the palmy days of monasticism in Roman Egypt. In course of time the monastic ideal reacted upon the secular clergy, and the monastic schools raised the level of learning throughout the duchy, until provincial councils succeeded in establishing the celibacy of the priesthood and the stricter discipline of Rome. In all this movement for reform the dukes took a leading part, inviting the reformers to their courts, aiding in the foundation and restoration of cloisters, and lending their strong support to the efforts for moral improvement in the secular clergy. They also asserted their supremacy over the Norman church, presiding in its councils, revising the judgments of its courts, appointing and investing its bishops and abbots. Moreover, while ready to coöperate with the moral ideas of the Papacy, they resisted all attempts at papal interference in Norman affairs. When Alexander II sought to restore an abbot whom William the Conqueror had deposed, the duke replied that he would gladly receive papal legates in matters of faith and doctrine, but would hang to the tallest oak of the nearest forest any monk who dared to resist his authority in his own land. William's resistance was equally firm in the case of Gregory VII, who failed completely in his efforts at direct action in William's dominions. Nowhere on the Continent, concludes Böhmer,[1] was there at this time a country where the prince and his

[1] *Kirche und Staat*, p. 41.

bishops were so energetic in the suppression of simony and violations of clerical vows; nowhere was the church so completely subject to the secular government.

The most prominent figure in the Norman church of the eleventh century, Odo, for nearly fifty years bishop of Bayeux, was far from fulfilling the stricter ideal of a prelate's life. Half-brother of the Conqueror through their mother Arlette, he received the bishopric as a family gift at the tender age of fourteen and became thereby one of the greatest princes of Normandy. His hundred and twenty knights' fees furnished him a body of powerful vassals; his demesne gave him manors and forests for the support of his household, fuel for his fires and reeds and rushes for his hall, rents and tithes at Caen and the monopoly of the mill at Bayeux, tolls and fines and market rights which produced a considerable income in ready money. For the invasion of England he is said to have offered a hundred ships, and he took an active part in the battle of Hastings, swinging a huge mace in place of spear and sword, since the shedding of blood was forbidden to an ecclesiastic. In the distribution which followed, Odo received large estates in the southeast, as well as the earldom of Kent and the custody of Dover Castle, and he seems to have ruled his lands with a heavy hand both as earl and as regent in William's absence. It even became his ambition to succeed the mighty Hildebrand as Pope, and he had already spent considerable sums at Rome when William, accusing him of tyranny and oppression, put him in prison, answering his assertion of ecclesiastical privilege with the statement that he imprisoned, not the bishop of Bayeux, but the earl of Kent. There he languished for five years till William on his death-bed, against his better judgment, released him for ten years more of rule in Normandy. Yet, though Odo's eulogists admit that he was given overmuch to worldly ambition, the lusts of the flesh and the pride of life, they tell us of his vigorous defence of his clergy by arms as well as by eloquence, of the young men of promise whom he supported in the schools of Lorraine and other centres of foreign learning, of the journey to Jerusalem on which he met his death, of the great cathedral which he built in honor of the Mother of God and adorned with gold and silver and probably with the very Bayeux Tapestry which is the chief surviving monument of his magnificence.

With the twelfth century the type changes. To the monastic historian a bishop like Philip d'Harcourt, likewise of the see of Bayeux, may appear wise in the wisdom of this world which is foolishness with God,[1] but his wisdom shows itself in frequent journeys to Rome and persistent litigation in the duke's courts, not in battles and sieges, and he owes his appointment to his influence as Stephen's chancellor and not to blood relationship. Arnulf of Lisieux is another royal officer, versatile, insinuating, shifty, anything but truthful if we may be-

[1] Robert of Torigni (ed. Delisle), I, p. 344.

lieve his fellow-bishops, but proud of his Latin style and his knowledge of law and prodigal of letters to the Pope. Their contemporaries continue to owe their promotion to service as chaplains or chancellors to the king, but they also have an eye toward Rome and must be canonists as well as secular officials. The contrast between Becket the king's chancellor and Becket the archbishop of Canterbury is symptomatic of the new age, although the conflict to which it led affected Normandy but indirectly. Relations with the lay power which once rested on local Norman custom come to be formulated in the sharper terms of the canon law of the universal church; appeals to Rome and instructions from Rome increase rapidly in volume and importance; the Norman clergy attend assemblies of the clergy of neighboring lands; and by the end of the Plantagenet period the Norman church is ready to be absorbed into the church of France.

Respecting the daily life and conversation of the cathedral and parish clergy the twelfth century is silent, save for the condemnations of particular evils in the councils of the province. From the middle of the thirteenth century, however, Normandy furnishes us, in the diary of visitations kept by the archbishop of Rouen, Eudes Rigaud, a picture of manners and morals which for authenticity and fulness of detail has probably no parallel in mediæval Europe; and one is tempted to carry back two or three generations his description of the canons of Rouen wandering about the cathedral and chatting with women during service, the nuns of Saint-Sauveur with their pet dogs and squirrels, and those of other convents celebrating the festival of the Innocents with dance and song and unseemly mirth, the monks of Bocherville without a Bible among them to read. It is hard to believe that there was anything new in the disorders which this upright archbishop chronicles place by place and year by year — ignorance, drunkenness, and incontinence among the parish and cathedral clergy, lax discipline, loose administration, and neglect of learning in the monasteries and nunneries. What was old in the time of Rabelais was probably old in the thirteenth century, and there is abundant evidence of abuses in the mediæval church, in Normandy and elsewhere. What we want most to know is how general these abuses were and how many there were to counteract them like Chaucer's ' povre persoun of a toun,' who taught "Cristes lore and his apostles twelve," but first "folwed it himselve." Data of this sort are always lacking in sufficient amount for any moral statistics, and they must be supplemented and interpreted by the evidence which has reached us of popular piety and devotion. Such are the processions of priest and people throughout the diocese to the cathedrals at Whitsuntide, the miraculous cures of disease by Our Lady of Coutances, and the extraordinary burst of contrition, religious enthusiasm, and zeal for good works which broke forth at the building of the spires of Chartres in 1145 and spread throughout the length and breadth of Normandy. Forming associations of those who confessed their sins, received penance, and reconciled themselves with their enemies, the faithful harnessed themselves to carts filled with stone, timber, food, and whatever might help the churches which they sought to serve, and drew them long miles until they seemed to fulfill the saying of the prophet, "the spirit of the living creature was in the wheels." The abbot of Saint-Pierre-sur-Dives, to whom we owe our fullest account of the movement, tells us of these processions:[1]

When they halt on the road, nothing is heard but the confession of sins and pure and suppliant prayer to God to obtain pardon. At the voice of the priests preaching peace hatred is forgotten, discord thrown aside, debts are remitted, the unity of hearts is established. But if any one is so far advanced in evil as to be unwilling to pardon an offender or obey the pious admonition of the priest, his offering is instantly thrown from the wagon as impure, and he himself is ignominiously and shamefully excluded from the society of the holy. There, as a result of the prayers of the faithful, one may see the sick and infirm rise whole from their wagons, the dumb open their mouths to the praise of God, the possessed recover a sane mind. The priests who preside over each wagon are seen exhorting all to repentance, confession, lamentations, and the resolution of a better life, while old and young and even little children, prostrate on the ground, call on the Mother of God and utter to her, from the depth of their hearts, sobs and sighs, with words of confession and praise. . . . After the faithful resume their march to the sound of trumpets and the

[1] The text is printed in the *Bibliothèque de l'École des Chartes*, XXI, pp. 120 *ff*.

display of banners, the journey is so easy that no obstacle can retard it. . . . When they have reached the church, they arrange the wagons about it like a spiritual camp, and during the whole of the following night the army of the Lord keeps watch with psalms and canticles, tapers and lamps are lighted on each wagon, and the relics of the saints are brought for the relief of the sick and the weak, for whom priests and people in procession implore the clemency of the Lord and his Blessed Mother. If healing does not follow at once, they cast aside their garments, men and women alike, and drag themselves from altar to altar . . . begging the priests to scourge them for their sins.

At the close of the Angevin period there were in Normandy something like eighty monasteries and convents, not counting the numerous cells and priories, as, for example, the various dependencies of the great abbey of Marmoutier at Tours. These were chiefly Benedictine foundations, though the newer movements of the Cistercians, Premonstratensians, and Augustinians were well represented, the only distinctively Norman order, the Congregation of Savigny, having been early absorbed by the Cistercians. The oldest of these establishments were at the two extremes of the duchy, Mont-Saint-Michel at one end and Jumièges, Saint-Wandrille, Saint-Ouen and Fécamp at the other; but the distribution was speedily equalized, and the great abbeys of the centre, Bec and Caen and Saint-Évroul, were soon known throughout Europe. The conquest of England opened a new field for monastic influence: twenty Norman monasteries had received lands in England by the time of the

Domesday survey, and the number was considerably greater when the holdings of alien priories were confiscated at the beginning of the fifteenth century. Mont-Saint-Michel, for example, had a priory in Cornwall as well as one at LeMans, and its lands in Maine, Brittany, and various parts of England did not allay its desire for more whenever opportunity offered. For a period of five years, from 1155 to 1159 inclusive, we have a record of the activity of its abbot, Robert of Torigni, in relation to the monastery's property, and a very instructive record it is. It takes him to England and the Channel Islands, to the king's assizes at Gavrai, Domfront, Caen, and Carentan, to the courts of the bishops of Avranches, Coutances, and Bayeux, and to that of the archbishop at Rouen; proving his rights, compromising, exchanging, purchasing, receiving by gift or royal charter; picking up here a bit of land, there a mill, a garden, a vineyard, a tithe, a church, to add to the lands and rents, mills and forests, markets and churches and feudal rights which he already possessed. There are also various examples of loans on mortgage, for the monasteries were the chief source of rural credit in this period, and as the land with its revenues passed at once into the possession of the mortgagee, the security was absolute, the annual return sure, and the chances of ultimate acquisition of the property considerable. With the resources of the monastery during his administration of thirty-two years Abbot Robert was able to increase the number of monks from forty to sixty, to enlarge the conventual buildings, in which he entertained the kings of England and of France, and to add a great façade to the abbey-church, a contribution to the massive pile of the Marvel which we are no longer privileged to behold. He also labored for the intellectual side of the monastery's life, restoring the library and enlarging it by a hundred and twenty volumes, and composing a variety of works on historical subjects which make him the chief authority for half a century of Norman history.

There is, however, not much concerning monasteries in Robert's chronicle, and even his special essay on the history of the Norman abbeys is confined to externals. Perhaps he was cumbered about much serving; more probably he saw nothing worthy of the historian's pen in the inner life of the institution. When the abbot had a new altar dedicated or renewed the reliquaries of St. Aubert and St. Lawrence, that was worth setting down, but the daily routine of observance was the same at Mont-Saint-Michel as in the other Benedictine foundations, and has remained substantially unchanged through the centuries of monastic history. At any rate no monkish Boswell has done for Normandy what Jocelin of Brakelonde did for contemporary England in that vivid picture of life at Bury St. Edmund's which Carlyle has made familiar in his *Past and Present*. A monk of Saint-Évroul, it is true, did a much greater thing in the

*Historia Ecclesiastica* of Ordericus Vitalis, but he was an historian, not a Boswell, and his experience of half a century of monastic life lies embedded deep in the five solid volumes of this wide-ranging work. One phase of the religious life of mediæval monasteries is admirably illustrated in Normandy, namely the mortuary rolls of the members and heads of religious houses. It early became the custom, not only to say prayers regularly for the departed members and benefactors of such a community, but to seek the suffrages of associated communities or of all the faithful. To that end an encyclical was prepared setting forth the virtues of the deceased and was carried by a special messenger from convent to convent, each establishment indicating the prayers which had there been said and adding the names of the brothers for whom prayers were solicited in return. The two most considerable documents of this sort which have come down to us are of Norman origin, the roll of Matilda, the first abbess of Holy Trinity at Caen, and that of Vitalis, founder of the Congregation of Savigny, which belongs to the year 1122 and is the oldest manuscript of this type extant in its original form, with all the quaint local varieties in execution. Each of these was carried throughout the greater part of England and of northern and central France, reaching in the first case two hundred and fifty-three different monasteries and churches, in the second two hundred and eight, and as the replies were often made at some length in prose or verse, they constitute a curious monument of the condition of culture in the places visited.

If the impulse toward religious reform in Normandy was of Burgundian origin, intellectual stimulus came chiefly from Italy. The two principal figures in the intellectual life of the duchy in the eleventh century, Lanfranc and Anselm, were Italians: Lanfranc distinguished for his mastery of law, Lombard, Roman, and canon, for the great school which he founded at Bec, and for his labors in the field of ecclesiastical statesmanship; Anselm his pupil and his successor as prior of Bec and as archbishop of Canterbury, remarkable as a teacher, still more remarkable as one of the foremost theologians of the Western Church. "Under the first six dukes," we are told, "there was hardly any one in Normandy who gave himself to liberal studies, and there was no master till God, who provides for all, sent Lanfranc to these shores." Teaching first at Avranches, Lanfranc established himself at Bec in 1042, and his school soon drew students from the remotest parts of France and sent them out in all directions to positions of honor and influence. Abbots like Gilbert Crispin of Westminster, bishops like St. Ives of Chartres, primates of Rouen and Canterbury, even a pope in the person of Alexander II, figure on the long honor-roll of Lanfranc's pupils at Bec. For an institution of such renown, however, we know singularly little concerning the actual course and methods of study at Bec, and its historian is compelled to fall back upon a general description of the *trivium* and *quadrivium* which made up the ordinary monastic curriculum. We do not even know whether Lanfranc actually taught the subject of law of which he was past master, though we can be sure that theology and philosophy had a large place under Anselm, and that the school must have felt the influence of the large part which its leaders took in the theological discussions of their time. An important form of activity in the monasteries of the period was the copying of manuscripts, a sure safeguard against that idleness which St. Benedict declared the enemy of the soul. Lanfranc sat up a good part of the night correcting the daily copies of the monks of Bec; the first abbot of Saint-Évroul had an edifying tale of an erring brother who had secured his salvation by voluntarily copying a holy book of such dimensions that the angels who produced it on his behalf at the judgment were able to check it off letter by letter against his sins and leave at the end a single letter in his favor! The monks of Saint-Évroul prided themselves on their Latin style, especially their Latin verse, and on their chants which were sung even in distant Calabria; yet the best example of their training, the historian Ordericus, freely admits the literary supremacy of Bec, "where almost every one seems to be a philosopher and even the unlearned have something to teach the frothy grammarians."

In the course of the twelfth century the leadership in learning passes from the regular to the secular clergy, and the monastic schools decline before the cathedral schools of Laon, Tours, Chartres, Orleans, and Paris, two of which, Paris and Orleans, soon break the bounds of the older curriculum and develop into universities. As the current of scholars sets toward these new centres, Normandy is left at one side; no longer a leader, its students must learn their theology and philosophy at Paris, their law at Orleans and Bologna, their medicine at Salerno and Montpellier. The principal Norman philosopher of the new age, William of Conches, the tutor of Henry II, is associated with Paris rather than with the schools of Normandy. Perhaps the most original work of the pioneer of the new science, the *Questiones naturales* of Adelard of Bath, is dedicated to a Norman bishop, Richard of Bayeux, but its author was not a Norman, nor do we find Norman names among those who drank deep at the new founts of Spain and Sicily.

For a measure of the intellectual activity of the Norman monasteries and cathedrals nothing could serve better than an examination of the contents of their libraries, where we might judge for ourselves what books they acquired and copied and read. This unfortunately we can no longer make. The library of Bec, partly destroyed by fire in the seventeenth century, was scattered to the four winds of heaven in the eighteenth, and while the legislation of 1791 provided for the transfer of

such collections to the public depositories of the neighboring towns, the libraries of Avranches, Alençon, and
Rouen, reënforced by the Bibliothèque Nationale, have
garnered but a small part of the ancient treasures of
Mont-Saint-Michel, Saint-Évroul, and the establishments of the lower Seine. Works of importance as well
as curiosities still survive — autograph corrections of
Lanfranc, the originals of the great histories of Robert
of Torigni and Ordericus Vitalis, service-books throwing
light on the origins of the liturgical drama, cartularies of
churches and abbeys, — but for a more comprehensive
view of the resources of the twelfth century we must
turn to the contemporary catalogues which have come
down to us from the cloisters of Saint-Évroul, Bec, Lire,
and Fécamp, and the cathedral of Rouen. After all, as
that delightful academician *Silvestre Bonnard* has reminded us, there is no reading so easy, so restful, or so
seductive as a catalogue of manuscripts; and there is no
better guide to the silence and the peace of the monastic
library, as one may still taste them in the quiet of the
Escorial or Monte Cassino. Let us take the most specific
example, the collection of one hundred and forty volumes bequeathed to Bec by Philip, bishop of Bayeux, at
his death in 1164, or rather the one hundred and thirteen which reached the monastery, twenty-seven having
fallen by the way and being hence omitted from the
catalogue. Like the other libraries of the time, this consisted chiefly of theology — the writings of the Fathers

and of the Carolingian and post-Carolingian commentators and theologians, ending with Philip's contemporaries, St. Bernard, Gilbert de la Porrée, Hildebert of Tours, and Hugh of St. Victor, and his metropolitan, Hugh of Amiens. Wise in the wisdom of this world, the bishop possessed the whole *Corpus Juris Civilis* in five volumes, as well as the leading authorities on canon law, Burchard, St. Ives, and the *Decretum* of Gratian. He had none of the Roman poets, although they were not unknown to Norman writers of his age, but a fair selection of prose works of a literary and philosophical character — Cicero and Quintilian, Seneca and the Younger Pliny, besides the mediæval version of Plato's *Timæus*. There is a goodly sprinkling of the Roman historians most in vogue in the Middle Ages, Cæsar, Suetonius, Valerius Maximus, Florus, Eutropius, and the Latin version of Josephus, besides such of their mediæval successors as came nearest to Anglo-Norman affairs. Science was confined to Pliny's *Natural History* and two anonymous treatises on mathematics and astronomy, while the practical arts were represented by Palladius on agriculture and Vegetius on tactics. On the whole a typically Norman library, deficient on the imaginative side, but strong in orthodox theology, in law, and in history; not in all respects an up-to-date collection, since it contained none of those logical works of Aristotle which were transforming European thought, and, save for a treatise of Adelard of Bath, showed no recognizable trace of the new science which was beginning to come in through Spain; strikingly lacking also, save for a volume on Norman history, in products of Normandy itself, even in the field of theology and scriptural interpretation, where, for example, Richard abbot of Préaux had written marvellous commentaries upon Genesis, Deuteronomy, Ecclesiastes, the Song of Songs, and the Proverbs of Solomon, and had "discoursed allegorically or tropologically in many treatises upon obscure problems of the Prophets." [1]

After all, works on the history of Normandy were the most Norman thing a Norman could produce, and it was in this field that the duchy made its chief contribution to mediæval literature and learning. All the usual types appear, local annals, lists of bishops and abbots, lives of saints, biographies of princes, but the most characteristic are the works in which the history of Normandy is grasped as a whole: the half-legendary account of the early dukes by Dudo of Saint-Quentin, the confused but valuable *Gesta* of William of Jumièges, at last restored to us in a critical edition,[2] the *Chronicle* of Robert of Torigni, and especially the great *Historia Ecclesiastica* of Ordericus Vitalis, the *chef-d'œuvre* of Norman historiography and the most important historical work written in France in the twelfth century.

Born in 1075 near Shrewsbury, Ordericus was early

[1] Ordericus Vitalis (ed. LePrévost), III, p. 431.
[2] Guillaume de Jumièges, *Gesta Normannorum Ducum* (ed. Marx), Société de l'Histoire de Normandie, 1914.

devoted to the monastic life, and lest family affection might interfere with his vocation and the sure hope of Paradise held out to the sobbing boy, his sorrowing parents sent him forever from their sight to spend his days at Saint-Évroul near the southern border of Normandy. Tonsured at ten, ordained a deacon at eighteen and a priest at thirty-two, he bore the burden and heat of the day under six successive abbots, until as an old man of sixty-six he laid down his pen with a touching peroration of prayer and thanksgiving to Him who had disposed these years according to His good pleasure. During this half century of poverty and obedience Ordericus had little opportunity to leave the precincts of the monastery, although on rare occasions we can trace him in England and at Cambrai, Rheims, and Cluni, and the materials of his history had to be gathered almost wholly from the well-stocked library of the abbey and from conversation with those who passed his way. These facilities were, however, considerable, for, remote as Saint-Évroul may seem in its corner of the *pays d'Ouche*, it was in constant relations with England, where it possessed lands, and with southern Italy, whither it had sent its members to found new convents; and like all such establishments it was a place of entertainment for travellers of all classes, priests and monks, knights and *jongleurs*, even a king like Henry I, who brought with them accounts of their journeys about the world and tales of great deeds in distant Spain, Sicily, and Jerusalem. There were few better places to collect materials for the writing of history, and there was no one who could make better use of them than Ordericus. He was fully launched in his great work by 1123, and he kept at it throughout the remaining eighteen years of his life, putting it aside in the winter when his fingers grew numb with the cold, but resuming it each spring in the clear round hand which meets us in many a manuscript of Saint-Évroul, and offering it at the end to future generations, a monument more lasting than the granite obelisk erected to his memory in 1912. His original purpose was limited to a history of his monastery, but the plan soon widened to include the principal movements of his time and finally grew to the idea of a universal history, beginning, indeed, with the Christian era instead of with the more usual starting-point of the Creation. Nevertheless, even in its final form the work of Ordericus is not a general history of the Christian centuries, for the general portion is chiefly introductory and comparatively brief; his real theme is Norman history, centring, of course, round the vicissitudes of his convent and the adjacent territory, but also giving a large place to the deeds of the Normans in that greater Normandy which they had created beyond the sea, in England, in Italy, and in Palestine. He is thus not only Norman but pan-Norman. The plan, or rather lack of plan, of his thirteen books reflects the changes of design and the interruptions which the work underwent; there is some repetition, much confusion, and a distinct absence of architectonic art. These defects, however, do not diminish the prime merit of the work, which lies in its replacement of the jejune annals of the older type by a full and ample historical narrative, rich in detail, vivid in presentation, giving space to literary history and everyday life as well as to the affairs of church and state, and constituting as a whole the most faithful and living picture which has reached us of the European society of his age. Neither in the world nor of the world, this monk had a ripe knowledge of men and affairs, independence of judgment, a feeling for personality, and a sure touch in characterization. He had also a Latin style of his own, labored at times rather than affected, ready to show its skill in well-turned verse or in well-rounded speeches after the fashion of the classical historians, but direct and vigorous and not unworthy of the flexible and sonorous language which he had made his own.

Latin, however, was an exclusive possession of the clergy, — and not of all of them, if we can argue from the examinations held by Eudes Rigaud, — and by the middle of the twelfth century the Norman baronage began to demand from the clerks an account of the Anglo-Norman past in a language which they too could understand. History in the vernacular develops in France earlier than elsewhere, and in France earliest in Normandy and in the English lands which shared the

Norman speech and produced the oldest surviving example of such a work, the *Histoire des Engles* of Gaimar, written between 1147 and 1151. The chief centre for the production of vernacular history was the court of that patron of ecclesiastical and secular learning, Henry II, and his Aquitanian queen, to one or both of whom are dedicated the histories of Wace and Benoît de Sainte-More. Wace, the most interesting of this group of writers, was a native of Jersey and a clerk of Caen who turned an honest penny by his compositions and won a canonry at Bayeux by the most important of them, his *Roman de Rou*. Beginning with Rollo, from whom it takes its name, this follows the course of Norman history to the victory of Henry I in 1106, in simple and agreeable French verse based upon the Latin chroniclers but incorporating something from popular tradition. Such a compilation adds little to our knowledge, but by the time of the Third Crusade we find a contemporary narrative in French verse prepared by a *jongleur* of Évreux who accompanied Richard on the expedition. If we ignore the line, at best very faint, which in works of this sort separates history from romance and from works of edification, we must carry the Norman pioneers still further back, to the *Vie de Saint Alexis* which we owe probably to a canon of Rouen in the eleventh century, and to the great national epic of mediæval France, the *Chanson de Roland*, pre-Norman in origin but Norman in its early form, which has recently been ascribed to Turold, bishop of Bayeux after the death of the more famous Odo and later for many years a monk of Bec. There is, one may object, nothing monastic in this wonderful pæan of mediæval knighthood, whose religion is that of the God of battles who has never lied, and whose hero meets death with his face toward Spain and his imperishable sword beneath him; but knights and monks had more in common than was once supposed, and we are coming to see that the monasteries, especially the monasteries of the great highways, had a large share in the making, if not in the final writing, of the mediæval epic as well as the mediæval chronicles.

When we reach works like these, the literary history of Normandy merges in that of France, as well as in that of England, which, thanks to the Norman Conquest and the Norman empire, long remained a literary province of France. We must not, however, leave this vernacular literature, as yet almost wholly the work of clerks, with the impression that its dominant quality is romantic or poetical. Its versified form was merely the habit of an age which found verse easy to remember; the literature itself, as Gaston Paris has well observed,[1] was "essentially a literature of instruction for the use of laymen," fit material for prose and not for poetry. It is thus characteristically Norman in subject as well as in speech — simple and severe in form, devout and

[1] *La littérature normande avant l'annexion*, p. 22.

edifying rather than mystical, given to history rather than to speculation, and seeking through the moralized science of lapidaries and bestiaries and astronomical manuals to aid the everyday life of a serious and practical people.

Normandy had also something to say to the world in that most mediæval of arts, architecture, and especially in that Romanesque form of building which flourished in the eleventh century and the first half of the twelfth. The great Norman churches of this epoch were the natural outgrowth of its life — the wealth of the abbeys, the splendor of princely prelates like Odo of Bayeux and Geoffrey of Coutances, the piety and penance of William the Conqueror and Matilda, expiating by two abbeys their marriage within the prohibited degrees, the religious devotion of the people as illustrated by the processions of 1145. The biographer of Geoffrey de Mowbray, for example, tells [1] us how the bishop labored day and night for the enlargement and beautification of his church at Coutances (dedicated in 1056), buying the better half of the city from the duke to get space for the cathedral and palace, travelling as far as Apulia to secure gold and gems and vestments from Robert Guiscard and his fellow Normans, and maintaining from his rents a force of sculptors, masons,

---

[1] *Gallia Christiana*, XI, instr., coll. 219–23; Mortet, *Recueil de textes relatifs à l'histoire de l'architecture* (Paris, 1911), pp. 71–75.

goldsmiths, and workers in glass. Nearly forty years later, when the church had been damaged by earthquake and tempest, he brought a plumber from England to restore the leaden roof and the fallen stones of the towers and to replace the gilded cock which crowned the whole; and when he saw the cock once more glistening at the summit, he gave thanks to God and shortly passed away, pronouncing eternal maledictions upon those who should injure his church. Of this famous structure nothing now remains above the ground, for the noble towers which look from the hill of Coutances toward the western sea are Gothic, like the rest of the church; and for surviving monuments of cathedrals of the eleventh and twelfth centuries we must go to the naves of Bayeux and Évreux and the St. Romain's tower of Rouen. Even here the impression will be fragmentary, broken by Gothic choirs and by towers and spires of a still later age, just as the simple lines of the early church of Mont-Saint-Michel are swallowed up in the ornate Gothic of the loftier parts of the great pile. Edifices wholly of the Romanesque period must be sought in the parish churches in which Normandy is so rich, or in the larger abbey-churches which meet us at Lessay, Cerisy, Caen, Jumièges, and Bocherville. Jumièges, though in ruins, preserves the full outline of the style of the middle of the eleventh century; Caen presents in the Abbaye aux Hommes and the Abbaye aux Dames two perfect though contrasted types of a few years later, the one simple and austere, the other richer and less grand. Freeman may seem fanciful when he suggests that these sister churches express the spirit of their respective founders, "the imperial will of the conquering duke" and the milder temper of his "loving and faithful duchess," [1] but in any event they are Norman and typical of their age and country. There are elements in the ornamentation of Norman churches in this period which have been explained by reference to the distant influence of the Scandinavian north or the Farther East, there are perhaps traces of Lombard architecture in their plan, but their structure as a whole is as Norman as the stone of which they are built, distinguished by local traits from the other varieties of French Romanesque to which this period gave rise. Not the least Norman feature of these buildings is the persistent common sense of design and execution; the Norman architects did not attempt the architecturally impossible or undertake tasks, like the cathedral of Beauvais, which they were unable to finish in their own time and style. "What they began, they completed," writes the Nestor of American historians in his sympathetic interpretation of the art and the spirit of *Mont-Saint-Michel and Chartres*. In Norman art, as in other phases of Norman achievement, the last word cannot be said till we have followed it far beyond the borders of the duchy, northward to Durham, "half house of God,

---

[1] *Norman Conquest*, III, p. 109.

half castle 'gainst the Scot," and the other massive monuments which made 'Norman' synonymous with a whole style and period of English architecture, and southward to those more ornate structures which Norman princes reared at Bari and Cefalù, Palermo and Monreale. "No art — either Greek or Byzantine, Italian, or Arab —" says Henry Adams,[1] "has ever created two religious types so beautiful, so serious, so impressive, and yet so different, as Mont-Saint-Michel watching over its northern ocean, and Monreale, looking down over its forests of orange and lemon, on Palermo and the Sicilian seas."

## BIBLIOGRAPHICAL NOTE

There is no general account of Norman life and culture in any period of the Middle Ages, and no general study of Norman feudalism. For conditions in France generally, see Luchaire, *La société française au temps de Philippe-Auguste* (Paris, 1909), translated by Krehbiel (New York, 1912); for England, Miss M. Bateson, *Mediæval England* (New York and London, 1904). On castles, see C. Enlart, *Manuel d'archéologie française*, II (Paris, 1904, with bibliography), and Mrs. E. S. Armitage, *The Early Norman Castles of the British Isles* (London, 1912). For William the Marshal, see Paul Meyer's introduction to his edition of the *Histoire de Guillaume le Maréchal* (Paris, 1891–1901); the poem has been utilized by Jusserand for his account of tournaments, *Les sports et jeux d'exercice dans l'ancienne France* (Paris, 1901), ch. 2.

The work of Delisle, *Études sur la condition de la classe agricole et l'état de l'agriculture en Normandie au moyen âge* (Évreux, 1851), is a classic.

---

[1] *Mont-Saint-Michel and Chartres*, p. 4.

The best studies of Norman municipal institutions are A. Chéruel, *Histoire de Rouen pendant l'époque communale* (Rouen, 1843); A. Giry, *Les Établissements de Rouen* (Paris, 1883–85), supplemented by Valin, *Recherches sur les origines de la commune de Rouen* (*Précis* of the Rouen Academy, 1911); Charles de Beaurepaire, *La Vicomté de l'Eau de Rouen* (Évreux, 1856); E. de Fréville, *Mémoire sur le commerce maritime de Rouen* (Rouen, 1857); Miss Bateson, *The Laws of Breteuil*, in *English Historical Review*, xv, xvi; R. Génestal, *La tenure en bourgage* (Paris, 1900); Legras, *Le bourgage de Caen* (Paris, 1911).

The excellent account of the Norman church in H. Böhmer, *Kirche und Staat in England und in der Normandie* (Leipzig, 1899), stops with 1154. On Odo and on Philip d'Harcourt see V. Bourrienne's articles in the *Revue Catholique de Normandie*, vii–x, xviii–xxiii. The register of Eudes Rigaud (ed. Bonnin, Rouen, 1852) is analyzed by Delisle, in *Bibliothèque de l'École des Chartes*, viii, pp. 479–99; the *Miracula Ecclesie Constantiensis* and the letter of Abbot Haimo are discussed by him, *ibid.*, ix, pp. 339–52; xxi, pp. 113–39. For the mortuary rolls, see his facsimile edition of the *Rouleau mortuaire du B. Vital* (Paris, 1909). The best monograph on a Norman monastery is that of R. N. Sauvage, *L'abbaye de S. Martin de Troarn* (Caen, 1911), where other such studies are listed. See also Génestal, *Rôle des monastères comme établissements de crédit étudié en Normandie* (Paris, 1901), and Delisle's edition of Robert of Torigni.

The schools of Bec are described by A. Porée, *Histoire de l'abbaye du Bec* (Évreux, 1901). Notices of the various Norman historians are given by A. Molinier, *Les sources de l'histoire de France* (Paris, 1901–06), especially ii, chs. 25, 33. For Ordericus and St. Évroul see Delisle's introduction to the edition of the *Historia Ecclesiastica* published by the Société de l'Histoire de France, and the volumes issued by the Société historique et archéologique de l'Orne on the occasion of the Fêtes of 1912 (Alençon, 1912). Other early catalogues of libraries, including that of Philip of Bayeux, are in the first two volumes of the *Catalogue général des MSS. des départements* (Paris, 1886–88). For the vernacular literature, see Gaston Paris, *La littérature normande avant l'annexion* (Paris, 1899); and L. E. Menger, *The Anglo-Norman Dialect* (New York, 1904). For the latest discussions of the *Chanson de Roland* see J. Bédier, *Les légendes épiques*, iii (Paris, 1912); and W. Tavernier's studies in the *Zeitschrift für französische Sprache und Lit-*

*teratur*, XXXVI–XLII (1910–14), and the *Zeitschrift für romanische Philologie*, XXXVIII (1914). Enlart, *Manuel d'archéologie française*, I, mentions the principal works on Norman ecclesiastical architecture. See also R. de Lasteyrie, *L'architecture religieuse en France à l'époque romane* (Paris, 1912), ch. 15; Enlart, *Rouen* (Paris, 1904); H. Prentout, *Caen et Bayeux* (Paris, 1909); Henry Adams, *Mont-Saint-Michel and Chartres* (Boston, 1913).

# VII

OF all the achievements of the heroic age of Norman history, none were more daring in execution or more brilliant in results than the exploits of Norman barons in the lands of the Mediterranean. Battling against the infidel in Spain, in Sicily, and in Syria, scattering the papal army and becoming the humble vassals of the Holy See, overcoming Lombard princes and Byzantine generals, the Normans were the glorious adventurers of the Mediterranean world throughout that eleventh century which constituted the great period of Norman expansion. Then, masters of southern Italy and Sicily, they put to work their powers of assimilation and organization and created a strong, well-governed state and a rich, composite civilization which were the wonder of Europe. If one were tempted to ascribe the successes of the Normans in England to happy accident or to the unique personality of William the Conqueror, the story of Norman achievement in the south, the work of scattered bands of simple barons without any assistance from the reigning dukes, would be conclusive proof of the creative power of the Norman genius for conquest and administration.

The earliest relations of the Normans with the countries of the Mediterranean were the outgrowth of those pilgrimages to holy places which play so important a part in mediæval life and literature. Originating in the early veneration for the shrines associated with the beginnings of Christianity and the sufferings and death of the Christian martyrs, pilgrimages were in course of time reënforced by the more practical motives of healing and penance, until the crowds of pilgrims who haunted the roads in the later Middle Ages included many a hoary offender who sought to expiate his sins by this particular form of good works. Sometimes these penitents would be sent to wander about the earth for a definite time, more frequently they would be assigned a journey to a neighboring shrine or to some more famous fountain of healing grace, such as Compostela, Rome, or Jerusalem. Compostela, hiding among the Galician hills the bones of no less an apostle than St. James the Greater, who became in time the patron saint of Spain and spread the name of Santiago over two continents, was early a centre of pilgrimage from France, and claimed as one of its devotees the mighty Charlemagne, the footsteps of whose paladins men traced through the dark defiles of the Pyrenees in the *Song of Roland*, as well as in the special itinerary prepared for the use of French pilgrims to the tomb of the saint. Rome was of course more important, for it claimed two apostles, as well as their living successor on the pontifical throne.

It needed no pious invention to prove that Charlemagne had been in Rome and had received the imperial crown as he knelt in St. Peter's, and men told how in their own time the great king Canute had betaken himself thither with staff and scrip and many horses laden with gold and silver. Already the number of strangers in Rome was so great that guide-books were compiled indicating its principal sights and marvels — "seeing Rome," we might call them —; and as the processions wound into sight of the Eternal City, they burst into its praise in that wonderful pilgrim's chorus: —

> O Roma nobilis, orbis et domina,
> Cunctarum urbium excellentissima,
> Roseo martyrum sanguine rubea,
> Albis et virginum liliis candida;
> Salutem dicimus tibi per omnia,
> Te benedicimus: salve per secula.

Jerusalem was most precious of all, by reason both of its sacred associations and of the difficulty of the journey. No Charlemagne was needed to justify resort to the Holy Sepulchre, where the mother of the great emperor Constantine had built the first shrine; but the great Charles had a hostel constructed there for Frankish pilgrims, and soon legend makes him, too, follow the road to Constantinople and Jerusalem, as we are reminded in the great Charlemagne window at Chartres. There were manuals for the pilgrim to Jerusalem also, but these were chiefly occupied with how to reach the heavenly city, though one of them contents itself with advising the traveller to keep his face always to the east and ask God's help.

In all this life of the road the Normans took their full share. Michelet would have it that their motive was the Norman spirit of gain, no longer able to plunder neighbors at home, but glad of the chance of making something on the way and the certainty of gaining a hundred per cent by assuring the soul's salvation at the journey's end. Certainly they were not afraid to travel nor averse to taking advantage of the opportunities which travel might bring. We find them, sometimes singly and sometimes in armed bands, on the road to Spain, to Rome, and to the Holy City. At one time it may be the duke himself, Robert the Magnificent, who wends his way with a goodly company to the Holy Sepulchre, only to die at Nicæa on his return; or a holy abbot, like Thierry of Saint-Évroul, denied the sight of the earthly Jerusalem which he sought, but turning his thoughts to the city not made with hands as he composed himself for his last sleep before a lonely altar on the shores of Cyprus. In other cases we find the military element preponderating, as with Roger of Toeni, who led an army against the Saracens of Spain in the time of Duke Richard the Good, or Robert Crispin half a century later, fighting in Spain, sojourning in Italy, and finally passing into the service of the emperor at Constantinople, where he had "much triumph and much victory." In this stirring world the line between pilgrim and adventurer was not easy to draw, and the Normans did not always draw it. Often "their penitent's garb covered a coat of mail," and they carried a great sword along with their pilgrim's staff and wallet.[1] We must remember that Normandy exported in this period a considerable supply of younger sons, bred to a life of warfare and fed upon the rich nourishment of the *chansons de gestes*, but turned loose upon the world to seek elsewhere the lands and booty and deeds of renown which they could no longer expect to find at home. The conquest of England gave an outlet to this movement in one direction; the conquest of southern Italy absorbed it in another.

In the eleventh century, as in the early nineteenth, Italy was merely a geographical expression. The unity of law and government which it had enjoyed under the Romans had been long since broken by the Lombard invasion and the Frankish conquest, which drew the centre and north of the peninsula into the currents of western politics, while the south continued to look upon Constantinople as its capital and Sicily passed under the dominion of the Prophet and the Fatimite caliphs of Cairo. Separated from the rest of Italy by the lofty barrier of the Abruzzi and the wedge of territory which the Papacy had driven through the lines of communication to the west, the southern half followed a

[1] Delarc, *Les Normands en Italie*, p. 35.

different course of historical development from the days of the Lombards to those of Garibaldi. Nature had thrust it into the central place in the Mediterranean world, to which the gulfs and bays of its long coast-line opened the rich hinterland of Campania and Apulia and the natural highways beyond. Here had sprung up those cities of Magna Græcia which were the cradle of Italian civilization; here the Romans had their chief harbors at Pozzuoli and Brindisi and their great naval base at Cape Miseno; here the ports of Gaeta, Naples, Amalfi, and Bari kept intercourse with the East open during the Middle Ages. And if the genius of Hamilcar and Hannibal had once sought to tear the south and its islands from Italy to unite them with a Carthaginian empire, their close relations with Africa had again been asserted by the raids and conquests of the Saracens, while their connection with the East made them the last stronghold of Byzantine power beyond the Adriatic. In the long run, however, it has been pointed out that, if the culture of this region came from the south, its masters have come from the north;[1] and its new masters of the eleventh century were to unify and consolidate it at the very time when the rest of the peninsula was breaking up into warring communes and principalities. In the year 1000 the unity of the south was largely formal. The Eastern Empire still claimed authority, but the northern region was entirely independent under

[1] Bertaux, *L'art dans l'Italie méridionale*, p. 15.

the Lombard princes of Capua, Benevento, and Salerno, while the maritime republics of Naples, Gaeta, and Amalfi owed at best only a nominal subjection. The effective power of Byzantium was limited to the extreme south, where its governors and tax-collectors ruled in both Apulia and Calabria. Of the two districts Calabria, now the toe of the boot, was the more Greek, in religion and language as well as in political allegiance, but its scattered cities were unable to defend themselves against a vigorous attack. The large Lombard population of Apulia retained its speech and its law and showed no attachment to its Greek rulers, whose exactions in taxes and military service brought neither peace and security within nor protection from the raids of the Saracens. There was abundant material for a revolt, and the Normans furnished the occasion.

The first definite trace of the Normans in Italy appears in or about the year 1016, when a band returning from Jerusalem is found at Monte Gargano on the eastern coast. There was here an ancient shrine of St. Michael, older even than the famous monastery of St. Michael of the Peril on the confines of Normandy with which it had shared the red cloak of its patron, and a natural object of veneration on the part of Norman pilgrims, who well understood the militant virtues of the archangel of the flaming sword. Here the Normans fell into conversation with a Lombard named Meles, who had recently led an unsuccessful revolt in Apulia

and who told them that with a few soldiers like themselves he could easily overcome the Greeks, whereupon
they promised to return with their countrymen and as-
sist him. Another story of the same year tells of a body
of forty valiant Normans, also on their way home from
the Holy Sepulchre, who found a Saracen army besieging Salerno and, securing arms and horses from the na-
tives, defeated and drove off the infidel host. Besought
by the inhabitants to stay, they replied that they had
acted only for the love of God, but consented to carry
home lemons, almonds, rich vestments, and other products of the south as a means of attracting other Normans to make their homes in this land of milk and
honey. Legend doubtless has its part in these tales, —
the good Orderic makes the twenty thousand Saracens
in front of Salerno flee before a hundred Normans! —
but the general account of the occasion of the Norman
expeditions seems correct. Possibly a Lombard emis-
sary accompanied the pilgrims home to help in the re-
cruiting; certainly in 1017 the Normans are back in
force and ready for business. There was, however,
nothing sensational or decisive in the early exploits of
the Normans on Italian soil. The results of the first
campaigns with Meles in northern Apulia were lost in a
serious defeat at Canne, and for many years the Normans, few in number but brave and skilful, sought
their individual advantage in the service of the various
parties in the game of Italian politics, passing from one

prince to another as advantage seemed to offer, and careful not to give to any so decisive a preponderance that he might dispense with them. The first Norman principality was established about 1030 at Aversa, just north of Naples, where the money of Rouen continued to circulate more than a century afterward; but such definite points of crystallization make their appearance but slowly, and the body of the Normans, constantly recruited from home, lived as mercenaries on pay and pillage. Their reputation was, however, established, and when the prince of Salerno was asked by the Pope to disband his Norman troop, he replied that it had cost him much time and money to collect this precious treasure, for whom the soldiers of the enemy were "as meat before the devouring lions." [1]

Among the Norman leaders the house of Hauteville stands out preëminently, both as the dominant force in this formative period and as the ancestor of the later princes of southern Italy and Sicily. The head of the family, Tancred, held the barony of Hauteville, in the neighborhood of Coutances, but his patrimony was quite insufficient to provide for his twelve sons, most of whom went to seek their fortune in the south, an elder group consisting of William of the Iron Arm, Drogo, and Humphrey, and a younger set of half-brothers, of whom the most important are Robert Guiscard and Roger. At the outset scarcely distinguishable from

[1] Aimé, *Ystoire de li Normant*, p. 124.

their fellow-warriors, *li fortissime Normant* of their historian Aimé, the exploits of these brothers are celebrated by the later chroniclers in a way which reminds us less of sober history than of the heroes of the sagas or the *chansons de gestes*. William of the Iron Arm and Drogo seem to have arrived in the south about 1036 and soon signalized themselves in the first invasion of Sicily and in the conquest of northern Apulia, where William was chosen leader, or count, by the other Normans and at his death in 1046 succeeded by Drogo, who was soon afterward invested with the county by the Emperor Henry III. It was apparently in this year that Robert Guiscard first came to Italy. Refused assistance by his brothers, he hired himself out to various barons until he was left by Drogo in charge of a small garrison in the mountains of Calabria. Here he lived like a brigand, carrying off the cattle and sheep of the inhabitants and holding the people themselves for ransom. On one occasion he laid an ambush for the Greek commandant of Bisignano whom he had invited to a conference, and compelled him to pay twenty thousand golden *solidi* for his freedom. Brigand as he was, Robert was more than a mere bandit. His shrewdness and resourcefulness early gained him the name of Guiscard, or the wary, and his Byzantine contemporary, the princess Anna Comnena, has left a portrait of him in which his towering stature, flashing eye, and bellowing strength are matched by his overleaping ambition and desire to dominate, his skill in organization, and his unconquerable will. Allied by marriage to a powerful baron of the south, he soon began to make headway in the conquest of Calabria, and while Drogo and his brother Humphrey were jealous of Robert's advancement, at Humphrey's death in 1057 he was chosen to succeed as count and leader of the Normans. Leaving to the youngest brother Roger, just arrived from Hauteville, the conquest of Calabria and the first attempts on Sicily, Guiscard gave his attention particularly to the affairs of Apulia, and after a series of campaigns and revolts completed the subjugation of the mainland by the capture of Bari in 1071. Five years after the battle of Hastings the whole of southern Italy had passed under Norman rule. The south had been conquered, but for whom? Robert was no king, and a mere count must have, for form's sake at least, a feudal superior. And this part, strangely enough, was taken by the Pope.

The relations of the Normans with the Papacy form not the least remarkable chapter in the extraordinary history of their dominion in the south. This period of expansion coincided with the great movement of revival and reform in the church which was taken up with vigor by the German Popes of the middle of the century and culminated some years later in the great pontificate of Gregory VII. So far as the Italian policy of the Papacy was concerned, the movement seems to have had two aspects, an effort to put an end to the disorders produced by simony and by the marriage of the clergy, evils aggravated in the south by the conflicting authority of the Greek and Latin bishops, and a desire to extend the temporal power and influence of the Pope in the peninsula. In both of these directions the conquests of the Normans seemed to threaten the papal interests, and we are not surprised to find the first of this vigorous series of Popes, Leo IX, interfering actively in the ecclesiastical affairs of the region and acting as the defender of the native population, which appealed to him and, in the case of Benevento, formally placed itself under his protection. Finally, with a body of troops collected in Germany and in other parts of Italy, he met the Normans in battle at Civitate, in 1053, and suffered an overwhelming defeat which clearly established the Norman supremacy in Italy. The Normans could not, however, follow up their victory as if it had been won over an ordinary enemy; indeed they seem to have felt a certain embarrassment in the situation, and after humbling themselves before the Pope, they treated him with respect and deference which did not prevent their keeping him for some months in honorable detention at Benevento. Plainly the Normans were not to be subdued by force of arms, and it soon became evident to the reforming party that they would be useful allies against the Roman nobles and the unreformed clergy, as well as against the dangerous authority of the German emperor. Accordingly in 1059, the year in which the college of cardinals received its first definite constitution as the electors of the Pope, Nicholas II held a council at the Norman hill-fortress of Melfi, attended by the higher clergy of the south and also by the two chief Norman princes, Richard of Aversa and Robert Guiscard. In return for the Pope's investiture of their lands, these princes took an oath of allegiance and fealty to the Holy See and agreed to pay an annual rent to the Pope for their domains; in Robert's oath, which has been preserved, he styles himself "by the grace of God and St. Peter duke of Apulia and Calabria and, with their help, hereafter of Sicily." As duke and vassal of the Pope, the cattle-thief of the Calabrian mountains had henceforth a recognized position in feudal society.

Guiscard, however, was not the man to rest content with the position he had won, or to interpret his obligation of vassalage as an obligation of obedience. He was soon in the field again, pushing up the west coast to Amalfi and up the east into the Abruzzi, taking no great pains as he went to distinguish the lands of St. Peter from the lands of others. The Pope began to ask himself what he had secured by the alliance, and a definite break was soon followed by the excommunication of the Norman leader. By this time the papal see was occupied by Gregory VII, who as Hildebrand had long been the power behind the throne under his predecessors, the greatest, the most intense, and the most uncompromising of the Popes of the eleventh century; yet even he

failed to bend the Norman to his will. Fearing a combination with his bitterest enemy, the Emperor Henry
IV, he finally made peace with Guiscard, and in the re-
newal of fealty and investiture which followed, the
recent conquests of the Normans were expressly ex-
cepted. No great time elapsed before the Pope was
forced to make a desperate appeal for Norman aid.
After repeated attempts Henry IV got control of Rome,
shut up Gregory in the Castle of Sant' Angelo, and in-
stalled another Pope in his place, who crowned Henry
emperor in St. Peter's. Then, in May, 1084, Guiscard's
army came. The emperor made what might be called 'a
strategic retreat' to the north, the siege of Sant' Angelo
was raised, and Rome was given over to butchery and
pillage by the Normans and their Saracen troops. Fire
followed the sword, till the greater part of the city had
been burned. Ancient remains and Christian churches
such as San Clemente were ruined by the flames, and
quarters like the Cælian Hill have never recovered
from the destruction. The monuments of ancient Rome
suffered more from the Normans than from the Van-
dals. Unable to maintain himself in Rome without a
protector, Gregory accompanied his Norman allies
southward as far as Salerno, now a Norman city, where
he died the following year, protesting to the last that he
died in exile because he had "loved justice and hated
iniquity." The year 1085 also saw the end of Robert
Guiscard. Sought as an ally alike by the emperors of

the East and of the West, he had begun three years earlier a series of campaigns against the Greek empire, seizing the ports of Avlona and Durazzo which were then as now the keys to the Adriatic, and battling with the Venetians by sea and the Greeks by land until his troops penetrated as far as Thessaly. He finally succumbed to illness on the island of Cephalonia at the age of seventy, and was buried in his Apulian monastery of Venosa, where Norman monks sang the chants of Saint-Évroul over a tomb which commemorated him as "the terror of the world": —

> Hic terror mundi Guiscardus; hic expulit Urbe
> Quem Ligures regem, Roma, Lemannus habent.
> Parthus, Arabs, Macedumque phalanx non texit Alexin.
> At fuga; sed Venetum nec fuga nec pelagus.[1]

With the passing of Robert Guiscard the half-century of Norman conquest is practically at an end, to be followed by another half-century of rivalry and consolidation, until Roger II united all the Norman conquests under a single ruler and took the title of king in 1130, just a hundred years after the foundation of the first Norman principality at Aversa. Guiscard's lands and title of duke passed to his son Roger, generally called Roger Borsa to distinguish him from his uncle and cousin of the same name. The Norman possessions in Calabria and the recent acquisitions in Sicily remained in the hands of Guiscard's brother Count Roger, nomi-

[1] William of Malmesbury, *Gesta Regum*, p. 322.

nally a vassal of the duke of Apulia, while the northern
principality of Capua kept its independence, to be subsequently exchanged for feudal vassalage. Roger of
Apulia, however, was a weak ruler, in spite of the good
will of the church and his uncle's support, and the revolt of his brother Bohemond and the Apulian barons
threatened the land with feudal disintegration. Want
of governance was likewise writ large over the reign of
his son William, who succeeded as duke in 1111 and ruled
till 1127. Guiscard's real successor as a political and
military leader was his brother Roger, conqueror and
organizer of Sicily and founder of a state which his
more famous son turned into a kingdom.

Once master of Calabria, Count Roger had begun to
cast longing eyes beyond the Straits of Messina at the
rich island which has in all ages proved a temptation to
the rulers of the south. No member of the house of
Hauteville, their panegyrist tells us, ever saw a neighbor's lands without wanting them for himself, and in
this case there was profit for the soul as well as for the
body if the count could "win back to the worship of the
true God a land given over to infidelity, and administer
temporally for the divine service the fruits and rents
usurped by a race unmindful of God." [1] The language
is that of Geoffrey Malaterra; the excuse meets us
throughout the world's history — six centuries earlier
when Clovis bore it ill that the Arian Visigoths should

[1] Geoffrey Malaterra, II, p. 1.

possess a fair portion of Gaul which might become his, six centuries later when Emmanuel Downing thought it sin to tolerate the devil-worship of the Narragansetts "if upon a Just warre the Lord should deliver them" to be exchanged for the "gaynefull pilladge" of negro slaves; [1] nor is the doctrine without advocates in our own day. We may think of the conquest of Sicily as a sort of crusade before the Crusades, decreed by no church council and spread abroad by no preaching or privileges, but conceived and executed by Norman enterprise and daring. Like the greater crusades in the East, it profited by the disunion of the Moslem; like them, too, it did not scruple to make alliances with the infidel and to leave him in peaceful cultivation of his lands when all was over.

The conquest of Sicily began with the capture of Messina in 1061 and occupied thirty years. It was chiefly the work of Roger, though Guiscard aided him throughout the earlier years and claimed a share in the results for himself, as well as vassalage for Roger's portion. The decisive turning-point was a joint enterprise, the siege and capture of Palermo in 1072, which gave the Normans control of the Saracen capital, the largest city in Sicily, with an all-anchoring harbor from which it took its name. The Saracens, however, still held the chief places of the island: the ancient Carthaginian strongholds of the west and centre, Eryx and 'inex-

[1] *Massachusetts Historical Society Collections*, fourth series, VI, p. 65.

pugnable Enna,' known since mediæval times as Cas-
trogiovanni; Girgenti, "most beautiful city of mortals,"
with its ancient temples and olive groves rising from the
shores of the African Sea; Taormina, looking up at the
snows and fires of Etna and forth over Ionian waters to
the bold headlands of Calabria; and Syracuse, sheltering
a Saracen fleet in that great harbor which had wit-
nessed the downfall of Athenian greatness. To subdue
all these and what lay between required nineteen years
of hard fighting, varied, of course, by frequent visits to
Roger's possessions on the mainland and frequent expeditions in aid of his nephew, but requiring, even when
the great count was present in person, military and
diplomatic skill of a high order. When, however, the
work was done and the last Saracen stronghold, Noto,
surrendered in 1091, Count Roger had under his dominion a strong and consolidated principality, where
Greeks and Mohammedans enjoyed tolerance for their
speech and their faith, where a Norman fortress had
been constructed in every important town, and where
the barons, holding in general small and scattered fiefs,
owed loyal obedience to the count who had made their
fortunes, a sharp contrast to the turbulent feudalism of
Apulia, which looked upon the house of Hauteville as
leaders but not as masters. Roger was also in a position
to treat with a free hand the problems of the church,
reorganizing at his pleasure the dioceses which had disappeared under Mohammedan rule, and receiving from

Pope Urban II in 1098 for himself and his heirs the dignity of apostolic legate in Sicily, so that other legates were excluded and the Pope could treat with the Sicilian church only through the count. This extraordinary privilege, the foundation of the so-called 'Sicilian monarchy' in ecclesiastical matters, was the occasion of ever-recurring disputes in later times, but the success of Roger's crusade against the infidel seemed at the moment to justify so unusual a concession.

At his death in 1101 Roger I left behind him two sons, Simon and Roger, under the regency of their mother Adelaide. Four years later Simon died, leaving as the undisputed heir of the Sicilian and Calabrian dominions the ten-year-old Roger II, who at the age of sixteen took personal control of the government. During the regency the capital had crossed the Straits of Messina from the old Norman headquarters in the Calabrian hills at Mileto, where Roger I lay buried; henceforth it was fixed at Palermo, fit centre for a Mediterranean state. When his cousin William died, Roger II was quick to seize the Apulian inheritance, which he had to vindicate in the field not only against the revolted barons but against the Pope, anxious to prevent at all cost the consolidation of the Norman possessions in the hands of a single ruler. Securing his investiture with Apulia from Pope Honorius II in 1128, Roger two years later took advantage of the disputed election to the Papacy to obtain from Anacletus II the dignity of king;

and on Christmas Day, 1130, he was crowned and anointed at Palermo, taking henceforth the title "by the grace of God king of Sicily, Apulia, and Calabria, help and shield of the Christians, heir and son of the great Count Roger." What this kingdom was to mean in the history and culture of Europe we shall consider in the next lecture.

Meanwhile, in order to complete our survey of the deeds of the Normans in the south, we must take some notice of the part they played in the Crusades and in the Latin East. A movement which comprised the whole of western Europe, and even made Jerusalem-farers out of their kinsmen of the Scandinavian north, could not help affecting a people such as the Normans, who had already served a long apprenticeship as pilgrims to distant shrines and as soldiers of the cross in Spain and Sicily. Three Norman prelates were present at Clermont in 1095 when Pope Urban fired the Latin world with the cry *Dieu le veut*, and they carried back to Normandy the council's decrees and the news of the holy war. The crusade does not, however, seem to have had any special preachers in Normandy, where we hear of no such scenes as accompanied the fiery progress of Peter the Hermit through Lorraine and the Rhineland, and of none of the popular movements which sent men to their death under Peter's leadership in the Danube valley and beyond the Bosporus. Pioneers and men-at-arms rather than enthusiasts and martyrs, the Normans kept their heads when Europe was seething with the new adventure, and the combined band of Normans, Bretons, and English which set forth in September, 1096, does not appear to have been very large. At its head, however, rode the duke of Normandy, Robert Curthose, called by his contemporaries 'the soft duke,' knightly, kind-hearted, and easy-going, incapable of refusing a favor to any one, under whom the good peace of the Conqueror's time had given way to general disorder and confusion. Impecunious as always, he had been obliged to pawn the duchy to his brother William Rufus in order to raise the funds for the expedition. With him went his fighting uncle, Odo of Bayeux, and the duke's chaplain Arnulf, more famous in due time as patriarch of Jerusalem. It does not appear that Robert was an element of special strength in the crusading host, although he fought by the side of the other leaders at Nicæa and Antioch and at the taking of Jerusalem. He spent the winter pleasantly in the south of Italy on his way to the East, so that he reached Constantinople after most of the others had gone ahead, and he slipped away from the hardships of the siege of Antioch to take his ease amidst the pleasant fare and Cyprian wines of Laodicea [1] — Robert was always something of a Laodicean! When his vows as a crusader had been fulfilled at the Holy Sepulchre, he withdrew from the stern work of

[1] Laodicea ad mare, not the Phrygian Laodicea of the Apocalypse.

the new kingdom of Jerusalem and started home, bringing back a Norman bride of the south for the blessing of
St. Michael of the Peril, and hanging up his standard in
his mother's abbey-church at Caen. Legend, however,
was kind to Robert: before long he had killed a giant
Saracen in single combat and refused the crown of the
Latin kingdom because he felt himself unworthy, until
he became the hero of a whole long-forgotten cycle of
romance.

The real Norman heroes of the First Crusade must be
sought elsewhere, again among the descendants of Tancred of Hauteville. When Robert Curthose and his
companions reached the south on their outward journey, they found the Norman armies engaged in the
siege of Amalfi under the great Count Roger and Guiscard's eldest son Bohemond, a fair-haired, deep-chested
son of the north, "so tall in stature that he stood above
the tallest men by nearly a cubit." The fresh enterprise caught the imagination of Bohemond, who had
lost the greater part of his father's heritage to his
brother Roger Borsa and saw the possibility of a new
realm in the East; and, cutting a great cloak into
crosses for himself and his followers, he withdrew from
the siege and began preparations for the expedition to
Palestine. Among those who bound themselves to the
great undertaking were five grandsons and two great-
grandsons of Tancred of Hauteville, chief among them
Bohemond's nephew Tancred, whose loyalty and prow-

ess were to be proved on many a desperate battle-field of Syria. Commanding what was perhaps the strongest contingent in the crusading army and profiting by the experience of his campaigns in the Balkans in his father's reign, Bohemond proved the most vigorous and resourceful leader of the First Crusade. His object, however, had little connection with the relief of the Eastern Empire or the liberation of the Holy City, but was directed toward the formation of a great Syrian principality for himself, such as the other members of his family had created in Italy and Sicily. As the centre for such a dominion Antioch was far better suited than Jerusalem both commercially and strategically, and Bohemond took good care to secure the control of this city for himself before obtaining the entrance of the crusading forces. He showed the Norman talent of conciliating the native elements — Greek, Syrian, and Armenian — in his new state, and for a time seemed in a fair way to build up a real Norman kingdom in the East. In the end, however, the Eastern Empire and the Turks proved too strong for him; he lost precious months in captivity among the Mussulmans, and when he had raised another great army in France and Italy some years later, he committed the folly of a land expedition against Constantinople which ended in disaster. Bohemond did not return to the East, and his bones are still shown to visitors beneath an Oriental mausoleum at Canosa, where Latin verses lament his loss to the cause of the Holy Land. Tancred struggled gallantly to maintain the position in Syria during his uncle's absence, but he fought a losing fight, and the principality of Antioch dwindled into an outlying dependency of the kingdom of Jerusalem, in which relation it maintained its existence until the line became extinct with Bohemond VII in 1287.

Two other Norman princes appear as leaders in the course of the later Crusades, Richard the Lion-Hearted, whose participation in the Third Crusade we have already had occasion to notice, and Frederick II, who succeeded to the power and the policy of his Norman ancestors of the south. For each of these rulers, however, the crusade was merely an episode in the midst of other undertakings; the day of permanent Frankish states in Syria had gone by, and neither made any attempt at founding a Syrian kingdom. The Fourth Crusade was in no sense a Norman movement, so that the Normans did not contribute to the new France which the partition of the Eastern empire created on the Greek mainland, where Frankish castles rose to perpetuate the memory of Burgundian dukes of Athens and Lombard wardens of the pass of Thermopylæ. In the Frankish states of Syria we find a certain number of Norman names but no considerable Norman element in the Latin population. The fact is that the share of the Normans in the First Crusade was out of all proportion to their contribution to the permanent occupation of the East. The principality of Antioch was the only Norman state in the eastern Mediterranean, and its distinctively Norman character largely disappeared with the passing of Bohemond I and Tancred. Unlike their fellow-Christians of France and Italy, the Normans were not drawn by the commercial and colonizing side of the crusading movement. The Norman lands in England and Italy offered a sufficient field for colonial enterprise, and the results were more substantial and more lasting than the romantic but ephemeral creations of Frankish power in the East, while the position of the Syrian principalities as intermediaries in Mediterranean civilization was matched by the free intermixture of eastern and western culture in the kingdom of Sicily.

## BIBLIOGRAPHICAL NOTE

The annals of the Norman conquest of southern Italy and Sicily are best given by F. Chalandon, *Histoire de la domination normande en Italie et en Sicile* (Paris, 1907), I. O. Delarc, *Les Normands en Italie* (Paris, 1883), is fuller on the period before 1073, but less critical. The Byzantine side of the story is given by J. Gay, *L'Italie méridionale et l'empire byzantin* (Paris, 1904); the Saracen, by Michele Amari, *Storia dei Musulmani di Sicilia* (Florence, 1854–72), III. There is nothing in English fuller than the introductory chapters of E. Curtis, *Roger of Sicily* (New York, 1912). Interesting historical sketches of particular localities will be found in F. Lenormant, *La Grande-Grèce* (Paris, 1881–84); and F. Gregorovius, *Apulische Landschaften* (Leipzig, 1877). On the sanctuary of St. Michael on Monte Gargano, see E. Gothein, *Die Culturentwickelung Süd-Italiens* (Breslau, 1886), pp. 41–111.

No study has been made of the Normans in Spain; for the pilgrimages to Compostela, see Bédier, *Les légendes épiques*, III. For the Normans in the Byzantine empire see G. Schlumberger, "Deux chefs normands des armées byzantines," in *Revue historique*, XVI, pp. 289–303 (1881).

There is nothing on the share of the Normans in the Crusades analogous to P. Riant, *Les Scandinaves en Terre Sainte* (Paris, 1865). The details can be picked out of R. Röhricht, *Geschichte des König-reichs Jerusalem* (Innsbruck, 1898), and *Geschichte des ersten Kreuz-zuges* (Innsbruck, 1901). There is no satisfactory biography of Robert Curthose; the legends concerning him are discussed by Gaston Paris in *Comptes-rendus de l'Académie des inscriptions*, 1890, pp. 207 *ff.* For the Norman princes of Antioch, see B. Kugler, *Boemund und Tankred* (Tübingen, 1862); and G. Rey's articles in the *Revue de l'Orient latin*, IV, pp. 321–407, VIII, pp. 116–57 (1896, 1900).

# VIII

## THE NORMAN KINGDOM OF SICILY

OF the widely separated lands which made up the greater Normandy of the Middle Ages, none have drifted farther apart than Norman England and Norman Sicily. Founded about the same time and not greatly different in area, these states have lost all common traditions, until the history of the southern Normans seems remote, in time as in space, from their kinsmen of the north. With the widening of the historical field, southern Italy and Sicily no longer occupy, as in Mediterranean days, the centre of the historic stage, and the splendor of their early history has been dimmed by earthquake and fever, by economic distress, and by the debasing traditions of centuries of misrule. Neither in language nor race nor political traditions does England recognize relationship between the country of the Black Hand and the 'mother of parliaments.' Yet if the English world has lost the feeling of kinship for the people of the south, it has not lost feeling for the land. It was no mere reminiscence of 'Vergilian headlands' and the thunders of the Odyssey that drew Shelley to the Bay of Naples, Browning to Sorrento, or, to take a parallel example elsewhere,

Goethe to the glowing orange-groves of Palermo. And it is not alone the poet whose soul responds to

> A castle, precipice-encurled,
> In a gash of the wind-grieved Apennine;

or

> A sea-side house to the farther South,
> Where the baked cicala dies of drouth,
> And one sharp tree — 't is a cypress — stands.

No land of the western Mediterranean has burnt itself so deeply into the imagination and sentiment of the English-speaking peoples. Twice has this vivid land of the south played a leading part in the world's life and thought, once under the Greeks, of "wind-swift thought and city-founding mind," as we may read in the marbles of Pæstum and Selinus and in the deathless pages of Thucydides; and a second time under the Norman princes and their Hohenstaufen successors, creators of an extraordinarily vigorous and precocious state and a brilliant cosmopolitan culture. If our interest in this brief period of Sicilian greatness be not Norman, it is at least human, as in one of the culminating points of Mediterranean civilization.

It must be emphasized at the outset that the history of this Norman kingdom was brief. It had two rulers of genius, Roger II, 1130–54, and his grandson Frederick II, 1198–1250, separated by the reigns of William the Bad and William the Good, — contemporaries of Henry II of England, and neither so bad nor so good as their names might lead us to suppose, — Tancred of Lecce and his son William III, and Constance, Roger's daughter and Frederick's mother, wife of the Hohenstaufen Emperor Henry VI. It is usual to consider the Norman period as closing with the deposition of William III in 1194 and to class Constance and Frederick II with the Hohenstaufen. In the case of Constance there seems to be no possible reason for this, for she was as Norman as any of her predecessors and issued documents in her own name throughout the remaining three years of her husband's life and during the few months of 1197–98 by which she survived him. With their son Frederick II, half Norman and half Hohenstaufen, the question is perhaps even, and the science of genetics has not yet advanced far enough to enable us to classify and trace to their source the dominant and the recessive elements in his inheritance. No one, however, can study him at close range without discovering marked affinities with his Norman predecessors, notably the second Roger, and the whole trend of recent investigation goes to show that, in the field of government as in that of culture, his policy is a continuation of the work of the Norman kings, from whom much of his legislation is directly derived. Half Norman by birth, Frederick was preponderantly Norman in his political heritage. It was in Sicily that he grew up and began to rule, and in Sicily that he did his really constructive work. To judge him as a Hohenstaufen is only less misleading than to judge him as a German king, for the centre and aim of his policy lay in the Mediterranean. In Frederick's sons, legitimate and illegitimate, the Norman strain is still further attenuated, and as they had no real opportunity to continue their father's work, it matters little whether we call them Normans or Hohenstaufen. The coming of Charles of Anjou ends this epoch, and his victory at Tagliacozzo in 1268 seals the fate of the dynasty. We may, if we choose, carry the Norman period to this point; for all real purposes it ends with the death of Frederick in 1250. The preceding one hundred and twenty years embrace the real life-history of the Norman kingdom. Brief as this is, it is too long for a single lecture, and we must limit ourselves to Roger and the two Williams, touching on the developments of the thirteenth century only in the most incidental fashion.

Throughout this period the territorial extent of the realm remained practically unchanged, comprising Sicily, with Malta, and the southern half of the Italian peninsula as far as Terracina on the western coast and the river Tronto on the eastern. There were of course times when the royal authority was disputed within and attacked from without, — feudal revolts, raids by the Pisans, expeditions of the German emperor, diplomatic contests with the Pope, — but it was not permanently limited or shorn of its territories. There were, on the other hand, moments of expansion, particularly by sea, for Sicily was of necessity a naval power and early saw the importance of creating a navy commensurate with its maritime position. The occupation of Tripoli and Tunis by Roger II seized the Mediterranean by the throat; the possession of Corfu threatened the freedom of the Adriatic; but neither conquest was permanent, and in the main the Greek empire and the powers of northern Africa succeeded in keeping the Sicilian kings within their natural boundaries.

In area about four-fifths the size of England, the southern kingdom showed far greater diversity, both in the land and in its inhabitants. Stretching from the sub-tropical gardens of Sicily into the heart of the highest Apennines, it was divided by mountain and sea into distinct natural regions between which communication continues difficult even to-day — the isolated valleys of the Abruzzi, the great plain of Apulia, the 'granite citadel' of Calabria, the rich fields of Campania, the commercial cities of the Bay of Naples and Gulf of Salerno, the contrasted mountains and shore-lands of Sicily itself. The difficulties of geography were increased by differences of race, religion, and political traditions. The mass of the continental population was, of course, of Italian origin, going back in part to the Samnite shepherds of primitive Italy, and while it had been modified in many places by the Lombard conquest, it retained its Latin speech and was subject to the authority of the Latin church. Calabria, however, was now Greek, in religion as in language, and the Greek element was considerable in the cities of Apulia and flowed over into Sicily, where the chief foreign constituent was African and Mohammedan. Politically, there was a mixed inheritance of Lombard and Roman law, of Greek and Saracen bureaucracy, of municipal independence, and of Norman feudalism, entrenched in the mountain-fortresses of upper Apulia and the Abruzzi; while the diverse origins of the composite state were expressed in the sovereign's official title, "king of Sicily, of the duchy of Apulia, and of the principality of Capua." The union of these conflicting elements into a single strong state was the test and the triumph of Norman statesmanship.

Plainly the terms of this political problem were quite different from that set the Norman rulers of England. Whatever local divergences careful study of Anglo-Saxon England may still reveal, there were no differences of religion or of general political tradition, while the rapidity of the conquest at the hands of a single ruler made possible a uniform policy throughout the whole country. The convenient formula of forfeiture and regrant of all the land, for example, created at once uniformity of tenure and of social organization. Moreover, as we have already seen, back of the Norman conquest of England lay Normandy itself, firmly organized under a strong duke, who took with him across the

Channel his household officers and his lay and spiritual counsellors to form the nucleus of his new central government, which was in many respects one with the central government of Normandy. In the south none of these favoring conditions prevailed. A country composed of many diverse elements was conquered by different leaders and at different times, so that there could be no question of uniformity of system. Indeed there could be no system at all, for the Normans came as individual adventurers, with no governmental organization behind them, and the instruments of government which they used had to be created as they went along. Whatever of Norman tradition reached the south could come only in the subdivided and attenuated form of individual influences. Furthermore, the Norman ingredient in the population continued relatively small. The scattered bands of early days were of course reënforced as time went on, but there was never any general migration or any movement that affected the mass of the population in town and country. If we had any statistics, we should doubtless find that some hundreds or at most a few thousands would cover the entire Norman population of Italy and Sicily. These brought with them their speech, their feudal tenures, probably some elements of Norman customary law; but, given their small numbers, they could not hope to Normanize a vast country, where their language soon disappeared and their identity was ultimately lost in the general mass.

Under such conditions there could be no general transplantation of Norman institutions. The rulers were Norman, as were the holders of the great fiefs, but, to speak paradoxically, the most Norman thing about their government was its non-Norman character, that is to say, its quick assimilation of alien elements and its statesmanlike treatment of native customs and institutions. The Norman leaders were too wise to attempt an impossible Normanization.

The policy of toleration in political and religious matters had its beginnings in the early days of the Norman occupation, but it received a broad application only in the course of the conquest of Sicily by the Great Count, and was first fully and systematically carried out by his son Roger II. In religion this meant the fullest liberty for Greeks, Jews, and Mohammedans, and even the maintenance of the hierarchy of the Greek Church and the encouragement and enrichment of Basilian monasteries along with the Benedictine foundations which were marked objects of Norman generosity. In law it meant the preservation of local rights and customs and of the usages of the several distinct elements in the population, Latin and Greek, Hebrew and Saracen. In local administration it involved the retention of the local dignitaries of the cities and the Byzantine offices of the *strategos* and the *catepan*, as well as the fiscal arrangements established by the Saracens in Sicily. And finally in the central government itself, the need of dealing wisely and effectively with the various peoples of the kingdom necessitated the employment of men familiar with each of them, and the maintenance of a secretarial bureau which issued documents in Greek and Arabic as well as in Latin.

It was in the central administration that Roger II faced his freshest problem, which was nothing less than the creation of a strong central government for a kingdom which had never before been united under a single resident ruler. His method was frankly eclectic. We are told that he made a point of inquiring carefully into the practices of other kings and countries and adopting anything in them which seemed to him valuable, and that he drew to his court from every land, regardless of speech and faith, men who were wise in counsel or distinguished in war, among whom the brilliant admiral George of Antioch is a conspicuous example. Nevertheless we should err if we thought of him as making a mere artificial composite. The Calabria of his youth had preserved a stiff tradition of Byzantine administration, and the Mohammedans of Sicily had an even stronger bureaucracy at work. Roger's capital was at Palermo, and it was natural that the Greek and Saracen institutions of Sicily and Calabria should prove the formative influences in his government as it was extended to the newly acquired and less centralized regions of the mainland. There was free adaptation and use of experience, but the loose feudal methods of the

Normans were profoundly modified by the bureaucratic traditions of the East.

The central point in the government lay, as in the states beyond the Alps, in the *curia* of feudal vassals and particularly in its more permanent nucleus of household officials and immediate advisers of the king. But whereas in the other parts of western Europe the feudal baronage still prevailed exclusively and gave way but slowly before the growth of specialized training and competence, the professional element was present in the Sicilian *curia* from an early period in the logothetes and emirs which Roger II had taken over from the earlier organization. The chancery, with its Latin, Greek, and Arabic branches, was inevitably a more complicated institution than in the other western kingdoms, and its documents imitated Byzantine and papal usage, even in externals. At one point, however, it shows close parallelisms with the Anglo-Norman chancery, namely in the free use of those *mandata* or administrative writs which are still rare in the secular states of the twelfth century; and if we remember that their employment constitutes the surest index of the efficiency of a mediæval administrative system, we must conclude, what is evident in other ways, that the most vigorous governments of the period were the two Norman kingdoms. In judicial matters the parallel is also instructive. Here a professional class had existed in the south from the outset as an inheritance from the Byzantine period, and it early makes its appearance in the *curia* in the person of a group of justices who in time seem completely to absorb the judicial functions of the larger body. At the same time the Norman barons were utilized for the royal justiciars which King Roger established throughout all parts of his kingdom. Parallel to these provincial justices ran provincial chamberlains, and over them there were later established master justices and master chamberlains for the great districts of Apulia and Capua, all subject to the central *curia*.

The fiscal system was especially characteristic. Roger's biographer tells us that the king spent his spare time in close supervision of the receipts and expenditures of his government, and that everything relating to the accounts was carefully kept in writing. Beginning with his reign we have documentary evidence of a branch of the *curia*, called in Arabic *diwan*, in Greek σέκρετον, and in Latin either *duana* or *secretum*, and acting as a central financial body for the whole kingdom. It kept voluminous registers, called in Arabic *defêtir*, and as its officers and clerks were largely Saracens, it seems plainly to go back to Saracenic antecedents. There are, however, some traces on the mainland of careful descriptions of lands and serfs like those which it extracted from its records in Sicily under the name of *plateæ*, so that Byzantine survivals should also be taken into account in studying the origin of the institution. Indeed this whole system presupposes elabo-

rate surveys and registers of the land and its inhabitants such as were made in the Egypt of the Ptolemies
and, less completely, in the Roman empire, and such as
meet us, in a ruder and simpler form, in that unique
northern record, the Domesday survey of 1086, itself
perhaps suggested by some knowledge of the older system in Italy. No one can fail to note the striking analo-
gies between the Sicilian *duana* and the Anglo-Norman
exchequer, but the disappearance of all records of the
southern bureau precludes any comparison of their
actual organization and procedure. The only parallel
records which have reached us are the registers of feudal
holdings, which exhibit noteworthy similarities in the
tenures of the two kingdoms.

Such feudal institutions were evidently a matter of
common inheritance, but any connections indicated by
similar administrative arrangements were doubtless
due to later imitation from one side or the other. Roger
II in Sicily and Henry I and Henry II in England were
at work upon much the same sort of governmental problem, and Roger was not alone in looking to other lands
for suggestions. Among the foreigners whom Roger
drew into his service we find Englishmen such as his
chancellor, Robert of Selby, and one of his chaplains
and fiscal officers, Thomas Brown, who later returned
to his native land to fill an honored place in the exchequer of Henry II. There was constant intercourse
between the two kingdoms in the twelfth century, and

abundant opportunity to keep one government informed of the administrative experiments of the other.

In general, however, the Sicilian monarchy was of a far more absolute and Oriental type than is found among the northern Normans or anywhere else in western Europe. The king's court, with its harem and eunuchs, resembled that of the Fatimite caliphs; his ideas of royal power were modelled upon the empire of Constantinople. The only contemporary portrait of King Roger which has reached us, the mosaic of the church of the Martorana at Palermo, represents him clothed in the dalmatic of the apostolic legate and the imperial costume of Byzantium, and receiving the crown directly from the hands of Christ; and a similar portrayal of the coronation of King William II shows that the scene was meant to be typical of the divine right of the king, responsible to no earthly authority. Theocratic in principle, the Sicilian monarchy drew its inspiration from the law-books of Justinian as well as from the living example on the eastern throne. The series of laws or assizes issued by King Roger naturally reflects the composite character of the Norman state. The mass of local custom is not superseded, the feudal obligations of the vassals are clearly recognized, influences of canon law and Teutonic custom are clearly traceable, indeed the northern conception of the king's peace may have been their starting-point; but the great body of these decrees flows directly from the Roman law, as preserved and modified by the Byzantine emperors. The royal power is everywhere exalted, often in phrases where the king is substituted for the emperor of the Roman original, and the law of treason is applied in detail to the protection of royal documents, royal coins, and royal officers. Even to question the king's ordinances or decisions is on a par with sacrilege.

The test of such phrases was the possession of adequate military and financial resources. Of the strength of King Roger's army his long and successful wars offer sufficient evidence; the great register of his military fiefs, the so-called *Catalogue of the Barons*, indicates that the feudal service could be increased when necessity demanded, while contingents of Saracen troops were as valuable to him as they had been to his father. Much the same can be said of his navy, for the safety of the Sicilian kingdom and its position in Mediterranean politics depended in large measure upon sea power, and Roger's fleet has a distinguished record in his Italian and African campaigns. Army and navy and civil service, however, rested ultimately upon the royal treasury, and among its contemporaries the Sicilian kingdom enjoyed a deserved reputation for great wealth. Its resources consisted partly in the products of the soil, such as the grain and cotton and peltry which were exported from Sicily itself; partly in manufactures, as in the case of the silk industry which King Roger developed in Palermo; and partly in the unrivalled facilities for trade which were presented by its many harbors and its advantageous location with respect to the great sea routes. Under the Norman kings the commerce of the southern kingdom was passive, rather than active, that is to say, it was carried on, not mainly by its own cities, such as Bari and Amalfi, which had enjoyed great prosperity in the Byzantine period and lost their local independence under the Normans, but by commercial powers from without — Pisa, Genoa, and Venice. The relative importance of each of these varied with the vicissitudes of Italian politics, but among them they shared the external trade of the kingdom. We find the Venetians on the eastern coast, the Genoese and Pisans at Salerno and the chief ports of Sicily, where they had special warehouses and often considerable colonies; and the earliest commercial records of Genoa and Pisa, notably the register of the Genoese notary, John the Scribe, enable us to follow their business from merchant to merchant and from port to port. Sicily served not only as a place for the exchange of exports for foreign products, the cloth of northern Italy and France and the spices and fabrics of the East, but also as a stage in the trade with the Orient by the great highway of the Straits of Messina or with Africa and Spain by way of Palermo and the ports of the western and southern coast. From all this the king took his toll. Without foregoing any of their feudal or domanial revenues or extensive monopolies, Roger and his successors tapped this growing commerce by port dues and by tariffs on exports and imports, thus securing their ready money from that merchant class upon which the future monarchies of western Europe were to build. The income from Palermo alone was said to be greater than that which the king of England derived from his whole kingdom.

It is evident, even from this brief outline, that the Sicilian state was not only a skilful blending of political elements of diverse origin, but also that it stood well in advance of its contemporaries in all that goes to make a modern type of government. Its kings legislated at a time when lawmaking was rare; they had a large income in money when other sovereigns lived from feudal dues and the produce of their domains; they had a well established bureaucracy when elsewhere both central and local government had been completely feudalized; they had a splendid capital when other courts were still ambulatory. Its only rival in these respects, the Anglo-Norman kingdom of the north, was inferior in financial resources and had made far less advance in the development of the class of trained officials through whom the progress of European administration was to be realized. Judged by these tests, it is not too much to call the kingdom of Roger and his successors the first modern state, just as Roger's non-feudal policy, far-sightedness, and diplomatic skill have sometimes won for him the title of the first modern king. This designation, I am well aware, has more commonly been reserved for the younger of Sicily's "two baptized sultans,"[1] Frederick II — *stupor mundi et immutator mirabilis*, "the wonder of the world and a marvellous innovator." No one can follow the career of this most gifted and fascinating figure without feeling the modern elements in his character and in his administration of the Sicilian state. His government stands ahead of its contemporaries in the thirteenth century as does that of Roger in the twelfth, and the more recent naturally seems the more modern. It is not, however, clear that the relative superiority was greater, and recent studies have made plain, what was not at first realized, that considerable portions of Frederick's legislation and of his administrative system go back to his Norman predecessors, some of them to Roger himself. After all it is not the historian's business to award prizes for being modern, especially when it is not always plain in what modernity consists. The main point is to recognize the striking individuality of the Sicilian state in directions which other states were in time to follow, and to remember that this individuality was a continuous thing and not a creation of the second Frederick. Moreover, as we shall shortly see, what is true in the field of government is also true in the field of civilization: the brilliant cosmopolitan culture of the thirteenth century is a direct development from similar conditions under King Roger.

[1] The phrase is Amari's: *Storia dei Musulmani di Sicilia*, III, p. 365.

The culture of the Norman kingdom was even more strikingly composite than its government. Both historically and geographically Sicily was the natural meeting-point of Greek, Arabic, and Latin civilization, and a natural avenue for the transmission of eastern art and learning to the West. Moreover, in the intellectual field the splendor of the Sicilian kingdom coincides with that movement which is often called the renaissance of the twelfth century and which consisted in considerable measure in the acquisition of new knowledge from the Greeks of the East and the Saracens of Sicily and Spain. Sicily was not the only channel through which the wisdom of the East flowed westward, for there were scholars from northern Italy who visited Constantinople and there was a steady diffusion of Saracen learning through the schools of Spain. Nowhere else, however, did Latin, Greek, and Arabic civilization live side by side in peace and toleration, and nowhere else was the spirit of the renaissance more clearly expressed in the policy of the rulers.

The older Latin culture of the southern kingdom had its centre and in large measure its source at Monte Cassino, mother of the Benedictine monasteries throughout the length and breadth of western Christendom. Founded by St. Benedict in 529, this establishment still maintains the unique record of fourteen centuries of monastic history and of more than forty generations of followers of the Benedictine rule, keeping age after age their vigils of labor, prayer, and fasting, but feasting their uncloistered eyes — *per gl' occhi almeno non v' è clausura!* — upon the massive ranges of the central Apennines and the placid valley of the Garigliano, "the Land of Labor and the Land of Rest." Its golden age was the eleventh and early twelfth centuries, when its relations with the Normans and the Papacy kept it in the forefront of Italian politics, when two of its abbots sat upon the throne of St. Peter, and when the greatest of them, Desiderius — as Pope known as Victor III — built a great basilica which was adorned by workmen from Constantinople with mosaics and with the great bronze doors which are the chief surviving evidence of its early splendor. Men of learning were drawn to the monastery, like the monk Constantine the African, skilled in the science of the Greek and Arabic physicians, whose works he translated into Latin. Manuscripts of every sort were copied in the characteristic south-Italian hand, the Beneventan script, which serves as a sure index of the intellectual activity throughout the southern half of the peninsula in this period — sermons and service-books, theological commentaries and lives of the saints, but also the law-books of Justinian and the writings of the Latin poets and historians with their commentators. Indeed without the scribes of Monte Cassino the world would have lost some of its most precious monuments of antiquity and the early Middle Ages, including on the mediæval side the oldest of the papal registers, that of John VIII, and on the classical, Varro, Apuleius, and the greater part of the works of Tacitus. Nowhere else is the work of the monasteries as the preservers of ancient learning more manifest.

The home of Greek learning in Italy was likewise to be found in monasteries, in those Basilian foundations which had spread over Calabria and the Basilicata in the ninth and tenth centuries and now under Norman protection sent out new colonies like the abbey of San Salvatore at Messina. Enriched with lands and rents and feudal holdings, they also set themselves to the building up of libraries by copies and by manuscripts brought from the East; but so far as we can judge from the ancient catalogues and from the scattered fragments which survive their dispersion, these collections were almost entirely biblical and theological in character, including however splendid examples of calligraphy such as the text of the Gospels, written in silver letters on purple vellum and adorned with beautiful miniatures, which is still preserved in the cathedral of Rossano.

Meanwhile, and largely as a result of the constant relations between southern Italy and the Greek East, learning had spread beyond monastery walls and ecclesiastical subjects, and had begun to attract the attention of men from the north. An English scholar, Adelard of Bath, who visited the south at the beginning of the twelfth century, found a Latin bishop of Syracuse skilled in all the mathematical arts, a Greek philosopher of Magna Græcia who discoursed on natural philosophy, and the greatest medical school of Europe in the old Lombard capital at Salerno, early famed as the city of Hippocrates and the seat of the oldest university in the West. A generation later, another Englishman, the humanist John of Salisbury, studies philosophy with a Greek interpreter in Apulia and drinks the heavy wines of the Sicilian chancellor; while still others profit by translations of Greek philosophical and mathematical works from the Italian libraries. The distinctive element in southern learning lay, however, not on the Latin side, but in its immediate contact with Greek and Arabic scholarship, and the chief meeting-point of these various currents of culture was the royal court at Palermo, direct heir to the civilization of Saracen Sicily.

The Sicilian court, like the kingdom, was many-tongued and cosmopolitan, its praises being sung alike by Arabic travellers and poets, by grave Byzantine ecclesiastics, and by Latin scholars of Italy and the north. A Greek archimandrite, Neilos Doxopatrios, produced at King Roger's request a *History of the Five Patriarchates* directed against the supremacy of the Pope of Rome; a Saracen, Edrisi, prepared under his direction the greatest treatise of Arabic geography,

celebrated long afterward as "King Roger's Book."
Under William I the chief literary figures are likewise
connected with the court: Eugene the Emir, a Greek
poet thoroughly conversant with Arabic and deeply
versed in the mathematics and astronomy of the an-
cients; and Henricus Aristippus, archdeacon of Catania
and for a time chief minister of the king, a collector of
manuscripts, a translator of Plato, Aristotle, and Dio-
genes Laertius, and an investigator of the phenomena
connected with the eruption of Etna in a spirit which
reminds us less of the age of the schoolmen than of the
death of the younger Pliny. Such a literary atmosphere
was peculiarly favorable to the production of translations from the Greek and Arabic into Latin, and we can
definitely connect with Sicily the versions which made
known to western Europe the *Meno* and *Phædo* of
Plato, portions of the *Meteorology* and of certain other
works of Aristotle, the more advanced writings of Eu-
clid, and the *Almagest* of Ptolemy, the greatest of ancient and mediæval treatises on astronomy. In a very
different field we have from Roger's reign a Greco-
Arabic psalter and an important group of New Testa-
ment manuscripts. "While we Germans were in many
respects barbarians," says Springer, "the ruling classes
in Sicily enjoyed the almost over-ripe fruits of an
ancient culture and combined Norman vigor of youth
with Oriental refinement of life." [1]

[1] *Bilder aus der neueren Kunstgeschichte*, I, p. 159.

There were lacking in the twelfth century the poetic and imaginative elements which flourished at the court of Frederick II, but on the scientific and philosophical sides there is clear continuity in the intellectual history of the south from Roger II and William to Frederick II and Manfred. At one point it is even probable that an actual material connection can be traced, for the collection of Greek manuscripts upon which Manfred set great store seems to have had its origin in codices brought from Constantinople to Palermo under the first Norman kings; and as Manfred's library probably passed into the possession of the Popes, it became the basis of the oldest collection of Greek manuscripts in the Europe of the humanists. Within its limits the intellectual movement at the court of King Roger and his son had many of the elements of a renaissance, and like the great revival of the fourteenth century, it owed much to princely favor. It was at the kings' request that translations were undertaken and the works of Neilos and Edrisi written, and it was no accident that two such scholars as Aristippus and Eugene of Palermo occupied high places in the royal administration. In their patronage of learning, as well as in the enlightened and anti-feudal character of their government, the Sicilian sovereigns, from Roger to Frederick II, belong to the age of the new statecraft and the humanistic revival.

The art of the Sicilian kingdom, like its learning and

its government, was the product of many diverse elements, developing on the mainland into a variety of local and provincial types, but in Sicily combined and harmonized under the guiding will of the royal court. Traces of direct Norman influence occur, as in the towers and exterior decoration of the cathedral of Cefalù or in the plan of that great resort of Norman pilgrims, the church of St. Nicholas at Bari; but in the main the Normans, in Bertaux's phrase, contributed little more than the cement which bound together the artistic materials furnished by others.[1] These materials were abundant and various, the Roman basilica and the Greek cupola, the bronze doors and the brilliant mosaics of Byzantine craftsmen, the domes, the graceful arches and ceilings, and the intricate arabesques of Saracen art; yet in the churches and palaces of Sicily they were fused into a beautiful and harmonious whole which still dazzles us with its splendor. The chief examples of this 'Norman' style are to be found at Cefalù, King Roger's cherished foundation, where he prepared his last resting-place in the great porphyry sarcophagus later transported to Palermo, and where Byzantine artists worked in blue and gold wonderful pictures of Christ and the Virgin and stately figures of archangels and saints of the Eastern Church; at Monreale, the royal mount of William II, commanding the inexhaustible wealth of Palermo's Golden Shell and

---

[1] *L'art dans l'Italie méridionale*, p. 344.

serving as the incomparable site of a great cathedral, with storied mosaics of every color covering its walls and vaulted ceiling like an illuminated missal, and with cloisters of rare and piercing beauty; and between them, in space and time, the palaces and churches of Palermo — the church of the Martorana, built in the Byzantine style and endowed with a Greek library by Roger's admiral George of Antioch, the Saracenic edifices of San Cataldo and San Giovanni degli Eremiti, and the unsurpassed glories of the Cappella Palatina — all set against the brilliant background of the Sicilian capital, which owes to the Norman kings its unique place in the history of art.

Welcoming merchants and strangers of every land and race, containing within itself organized communities of Greeks, Mohammedans, and Jews, each with its own churches, mosques, or synagogues, the Palermo of the twelfth century was a great cosmopolitan city and the natural centre of a Mediterranean art. Midway between Cordova and Constantinople, between Africa and Italy, it laid them all under contribution. Travellers celebrated the luxuriant gardens of the city and its surrounding plain, with the vast fields of sugar cane and groves of orange, fig, and lemon, olive and palm and pomegranate, its commodious harbor and its spacious and busy streets, its gorgeous fabrics and abundance of foreign wares, its walls and palaces and places of worship. "A stupendous city," says the Spanish traveller,

Ibn Giobair,[1] "elegant, graceful, and splendid, rising before one like a temptress" . . . and offering its king — "may Allah take them from him! — every pleasure in the world." An artist's city, too, distinguished by the qualities which Goethe saw in it, "the purity of its light, the delicacy of its lines and tones, the harmony of earth and sea and sky."

From the highest point in the capital rose the royal palace, which still retains, in spite of the transformations of eight centuries, something of the massiveness and the splendor of its Norman original, of which it preserves the great Pisan tower, — once the repository of the royal treasure, — the royal chapel, and one of the state apartments of King Roger's time. Its terraces and gardens have long since disappeared, with their marble lions and plashing fountains which resembled the Alhambra or the great pleasure-grounds of the Mohammedan East; but we can easily call them to life with the aid of the Saracen poets and of the remains of the other royal residences which surrounded the city "like a necklace of pearls." Here, amid his harem and his eunuchs, the officers of his court and his retinue of Mohammedan servants, the king lived much after the manner of an Oriental potentate. On state occasions he donned the purple and gold of the Greek emperors or the sumptuous vestments of red samite, embroidered

[1] His description is translated by Amari, *Biblioteca arabo-sicula* (Turin, 1888), I, pp. 155 *ff.;* and by Schiaparelli, *Ibn Gubayr* (Rome, 1906), pp. 328 *ff.* Cf. Waern, *Mediæval Sicily*, pp. 64 *ff.*

with golden tigers and camels and Arabic invocations to the Christian Redeemer, which are still preserved among the treasures of the Holy Roman Empire at Vienna. And when, on festivals, he entered the palace chapel, Latin in its ground-plan, Greek and Arabic in its ornamentation, the atmosphere was likewise Oriental. As described at its dedication in 1140, with the starry heavens of its ceiling and the flowery meadows of its pavement, the chapel preserves its fundamental features to-day. Dome and choir are dominated by great Byzantine figures of Christ, accompanied by Byzantine saints and scenes with Greek inscriptions, all executed with the fullest brilliancy of which mosaics are capable, while the stalactite ceiling, "dripping with all the elaborate richness of Saracen art," seems "to re-create some forgotten vision of the *Arabian Nights*." Harmonious in design yet infinitely varied in detail, rich beyond belief in color and in line, reflecting alike the dim rays of its pendent lamps or the full light of the southern sun, the Cappella Palatina is the fullest and most adequate expression of the many-sided art of the Norman kingdom and the unifying force of the Norman kings.

Brilliant but ephemeral, precocious but lacking in permanent results — such are the judgments commonly passed upon the Sicilian kingdom and its civilization. At best the kingdom seems to reach no farther than Frederick II, and of him Freeman has said that, though qualified by genius to start some great movement or begin some new era, he seemed fated to stand at the end of everything which he touched — the mediæval empire, the Sicilian kingdom, the Norman-Hohenstaufen line.[1] In the field of government these statements are in the main true: the rapid changes of dynasties and the deep political decline into which the south ultimately fell destroyed the unity of its political development and nullified the work of Norman statebuilding, so that the enduring results of Norman statesmanship and Norman law must be sought in the north and not in Italy. That, however, is not the whole of the story, and in the field of culture influences less palpable, but none the less real, flowed from the Norman stream into the general currents of European civilization. So long as the Renaissance of the fourteenth and fifteenth centuries was looked upon as simply the negation of the Middle Ages by a return to classical antiquity, figures such as King Roger and Frederick II were merely 'sports,' isolated flashes of genius and modernity without any relation to their own times or to the greater movement which followed. Since, however, we have come to view the Renaissance in its larger aspects as far more than a classical revival, its relations to the Middle Ages are seen to have been much more intimate

[1] "The Emperor Frederick the Second," in *Historical Essays*, first series, p. 291.

and important than was once supposed. The evolution is at times rapid, but the *Trecento* grows out of the centuries which preceded as naturally as it grew into the *Quattrocento* which followed. The place of Italy in this process is universally recognized; the place of southern Italy is sometimes overlooked. We are too prone to forget that Niccola Pisano was also called Nicholas of Apulia; that Petrarch owed much to his sojourn at the Neapolitan court; that Boccaccio learned his Greek from a Calabrian; that the first notes of a new Italian literature were sounded at the court of Frederick II. Many phases of the relation between south and north in this transitional period are still obscure, but of the significance of the southern contribution there is now reasonable assurance. Moreover, the continuity between the intellectual movement under Roger and William I and that under Frederick II and later can be followed in some detail in the history of individual manuscripts and authors. When humanists like Petrarch and Salutati read Plato's *Phædo* or Ptolemy's *Almagest*, their libraries show that they used the Latin versions of the Sicilian translators of the twelfth century. The learning of the southern kingdom may have been a faint light, but it was handed on, not extinguished.

For our general understanding of the Normans and their work, it is well that we should trace them in the lands where their direct influence grows faint and dim, as well as in those where their descendants still rule. Only a formal and mechanical view of history seeks to ticket off particular races against particular regions as the sole sources of population and power; only false national pride conceives of any people as continually in the vanguard of civilization. Races are mixed things, institutions and civilization are still more complex, and no people can claim to be a unique and permanent source of light and strength. Outside of Normandy the Normans were but a small folk, and sooner or later they inevitably lost their identity. They did their work pre-eminently not as a people apart, but as a group of leaders and energizers, the little leaven that leaveneth the whole lump. Wherever they went, they showed a marvellous power of initiative and of assimilation; if the initiative is more evident in England, the assimilation is more manifest in Sicily. The penalty for such activity is rapid loss of identity; the reward is a large share in the general development of civilization. If the Normans paid the penalty, they also reaped the reward, and they were never more Norman than in adopting the statesmanlike policy of toleration and assimilation which led to their ultimate extinction. *Plus ça change, plus c'est la même chose!*

## BIBLIOGRAPHICAL NOTE

The best general account of the Norman kingdom is that of Chalandon, who carries its history to 1194 and gives also a provisional description of its institutions and an unsatisfactory chapter on its civilization. E. Caspar, *Roger II* (Innsbruck, 1904), is the best book on the reign; Curtis, *Roger of Sicily*, is convenient. G. B. Siragusa, *Il regno di Guglielmo I* (Palermo, 1885–86), and I. La Lumia, *Storia della Sicilia sotto Guglielmo il Buono* (Florence, 1867), need revision. For Constance, T. Toeche, *Kaiser Heinrich VI* (Leipzig, 1867), is still useful.

The treatment of Sicilian institutions by E. Mayer, *Italienische Verfassungsgeschichte* (Leipzig, 1909), is too juristic. There is an excellent book on the chancery by K. A. Kehr, *Die Urkunden der normannisch-sicilischen Könige* (Innsbruck, 1902); and on the *duana* there are important monographs by Amari, in the *Memorie dei Lincei*, third series, II, pp. 409–38 (1878); and by C. A. Garufi, in *Archivio storico italiano*, fifth series, XXVII, pp. 225–63 (1901). For local administration see the valuable study of Miss E. Jamison, *The Norman Administration of Apulia and Capua*, in *Papers of the British School at Rome*, VI, pp. 211–481 (1913). See also H. Niese, *Die Gesetzgebung der normannischen Dynastie im Regnum Siciliae* (Halle, 1910); Haskins, "England and Sicily in the Twelfth Century," in *English Historical Review*, XXVI, pp. 433–47, 641–65 (1911); W. Cohn, *Die Geschichte der normannisch-sicilischen Flotte* (Breslau, 1910); R. Straus, *Die Juden im Königreich Sizilien* (Heidelberg, 1910); F. Zechbauer, *Das mittelalterliche Strafrecht Siziliens* (Berlin, 1908); and various studies in the *Miscellanea Salinas* (Palermo, 1907) and the *Centenario Michele Amari* (Palermo, 1910). The commerce of the Sicilian kingdom is described by A. Schaube, *Handelsgeschichte der romanischen Völker* (Munich, 1906).

For Monte Cassino in this period see E. A. Loew, *The Beneventan Script* (Oxford, 1914), with the works there cited; R. Palmarocchi, *L'abbazia di Montecassino e la conquista normanna* (Rome, 1913). On the Greek monasteries, see Gay, *L'Italie méridionale;* P. Batiffol, *L'abbaye de Rossano* (Paris, 1891); K. Lake, "The Greek Monasteries in South Italy," in *Journal of Theological Studies*, IV, V (1903–04); and F. LoParco, *Scolario-Saba*, in *Atti* of the Naples Academy, new series, I (1910). The best account of Saracen culture in Sicily is still that of Amari. On the south-Italian and Sicilian translators, see O. Hartwig, "Die Uebersetzungsliteratur Unteritaliens in der normannisch-staufischen Epoche," in *Centralblatt für Bibliothekswesen*, III, pp. 161–90, 223–25, 505 (1886); Haskins and Lockwood, *The Sicilian Translators of the Twelfth Century and the First Latin Version of Ptolemy's Almagest*, in *Harvard Studies in Classical Philology*, XXI, pp. 75–102 (1910); Haskins, *ibid.*, XXIII, pp. 155–166; XXV, pp. 87–105. On the Sicilian origin of the Greek MSS. of the papal library, see J. L. Heiberg, in *Oversigt* of the Danish Academy, 1891, pp. 305–18; F. Ehrle, in *Festgabe Anton de Waal* (Rome, 1913), pp. 348–51. The connection of the intellectual movement of the twelfth century with the renaissance under Frederick II is well brought out by Niese, "Zur Geschichte des geistigen Lebens am Hofe Kaiser Friedrichs II," in *Historische Zeitschrift*, CVIII, pp. 473–540 (1912). In general see F. Novati, *Le origini*, in course of publication in the *Storia letteraria d'Italia* (Milan, since 1897).

The development of art in the south in this period is treated by A. Venturi, *Storia dell' arte italiana* (Rome, 1901 ff.), II, ch. 3; III, ch. 2. See also C. Diehl, *L'art byzantin dans l'Italie méridionale* (Paris, 1894). For the continental territories there is an excellent account in E. Bertaux, *L'art dans l'Italie méridionale* (Paris, 1904). There is nothing so good for Sicily, although there are monographs on particular edifices. Diehl, *Palerme et Syracuse* (Paris, 1907), is a good sketch with illustrations; Miss C. Waern, *Mediæval Sicily* (London, 1910), is more popular. Freeman has a readable essay on "The Normans at Palermo," in his *Historical Essays*, third series, pp. 437–76. See also A. Springer, "Die mittelalterliche Kunst in Palermo," in his *Bilder aus der neueren Kunstgeschichte* (Bonn, 1886), I, pp. 157–208; and A. Goldschmidt, "Die normannischen Königspaläste in Palermo," in *Zeitschrift für Bauwesen*, XLVIII, coll. 541–90 (1898). Interesting aspects of twelfth-century Palermo are depicted in the Bern codex of Peter of Eboli, reproduced by Siragusa for the Istituto Storico Italiano (1905) and by Rota for the new edition of Muratori (1904–10). Surviving portions of the royal costume are reproduced by F. Bock, *Die Kleinodien des heil.-römischen Reiches* (Vienna, 1864).

# INDEX